CODE NAME CAMILLE

A STORY OF TRUST, LOVE AND BETRAYAL

KATHRYN GAUCI

Code Name Camille was first published in the **USA Today** Best Seller, ***The Darkest Hour: WWII Tales of Resistance*** Inspired by the brave actions of men, women, and adolescents who fought against the occupying Axis powers around the world,

All proceeds were donated to The United States Holocaust Memorial Museum in Washington, DC

CHAPTER ONE

Sometime around 6:00 pm on a wet, autumn day in 1942, twenty-one-year-old Nathalie Fontaine arrived at Paris's Gare Montparnasse. The journey from her hometown near the Pyrénées had taken just over three days. Finally, she had made it. Paris, the city of lights; a place she had wanted to visit for as long as she could remember, albeit under different circumstances. She was cold, exhausted, and hungry, and she had one thing on her mind – to join the Résistance and rid her country of its Nazi occupiers.

As she stepped down from the carriage with her suitcase, she had no idea what that would entail. Such is the idealism of youth. But she did have a name and address; her only contact in Paris, and it was this that she pinned her hopes on. Filled with travellers, guards, German soldiers, and the Gestapo, the station looked identical to the other major railway stops she had passed through. At Montparnasse, they were out in force, checking identity papers and hauling terrified people away on a whim. The look on the people's faces spoke volumes. Paris was under siege, a city where its inhabitants lived in the shadow of German oppression

A man with a tanned complexion, clad in a dark grey overcoat and fedora, asked to see her documents. She gave him a sweet smile and handed them to him. After a thorough check, he returned them, minus the smile, and indicated for her to move on. She breathed out a sigh of relief. How she loathed these people. Yet despite her parents' reluctance to allow her to leave, it was little things like this that spurred her on. She knew she'd made the right decision.

Outside the station, she stopped to get her bearings and headed for the metro in the direction of Pont de l'Alma. An hour later she arrived at rue Frédéric Chopin, a pretty street of elegant 19th century buildings with slate grey roofs, a short five-minute walk from the bridge. It was now dark and most of the shops had closed, except for one, a florist – *La Vie en Fleurs*. She checked the address – 29 rue Frédéric Chopin. She had reached her destination.

Outside the shop, underneath a green and white striped awning, stood a colourful display of baskets and rustic boxes of cut flowers and plants. A row of light-bulbs, strung up under the awning, twinkled through the soft rain, casting a warm glow over the blooms. A picture-perfect setting: romantic, serene, and inviting. The door opened and a slim woman in her late fifties, her hair tied back in a neat roll, came out and started to clear away the flowers with as much care as the display she had created. Nathalie crossed the road towards her. When the woman heard the footsteps on the cobblestones, she turned to look.

'Mme Reynaud?' asked Nathalie.

A huge smile crossed the woman's face. She knew immediately who the stranger was.

'Thank God!' she replied, relieved to see her, and gave her a warm welcoming hug. 'We expected you yesterday. When you didn't turn up, we started to imagine all sorts of things.'

'There were disruptions on the lines. You know how things are,' Nathalie answered.

Mme Reynaud took her suitcase from her and ushered her inside the shop, filled with more flowers, vases, the odd sculpture, and ribbons of various thickness and colours. There was barely enough room to swing a cat around.

'Antoine!' she called out through a curtain that led to a back room. 'Our visitor has arrived.'

A man appeared and shook her hand. 'Welcome to Paris, Nathalie. It's good to have you with us.'

Antoine Reynaud was a stout man who walked with a limp. Nathalie guessed that he was at least ten years older than his petite wife.

'Give the girl something to eat,' he said to his wife, 'while I bring everything inside and close the shop.'

Nathalie followed Mme Reynaud into the back room.

'Here, give me your coat,' she said. 'It's wet through. You'll catch your death of cold.'

She shook it and hung it on a peg next to the wood heater and added another log on the fire, sending out a streak of orange flames and a cloud of smoke.

'The wood has not had time to dry,' she said, holding a handkerchief over her nose and mouth whilst wafting the smoke away with the other hand. 'We are fortunate to have this.'

Nathalie thought of her home near the Pyrénées. Being a village house, it didn't have too many luxuries, but it did have a large barn at the back of the house which was always filled with wood for the cold winters. It was only autumn and already firewood seemed to be in short supply here. How bad would it be during winter?

Mme Reynaud cut a thick slice of hot beef and placed it on a plate alongside a generous helping of braised carrots and leeks. The only thing Nathalie had eaten in three days was a dried sausage, a piece of hard cheese and bread. Now famished, she ate it in no time. Mme Reynaud gave her more.

'We're going to have to fatten you up,' she laughed. 'Paris in winter under occupation is not the best place to be. You will need all your strength.'

Antoine reappeared. 'Tell, me, how is your father?' he asked. 'I haven't seen him in years.'

Antoine Reynaud was her father's uncle and it was partly due to him that Nathalie had come to Paris. When the Germans occupied the city, they wasted no time in rounding up anyone who stepped out of line. Antoine and Madeleine Reynaud suddenly found themselves hiding friends who had been outspoken about Pétain and the Vichy government's collaboration with the Nazis. Within a short space of time, it became clear that these people were being detained and tortured. They had to escape as soon as possible, and plans were put into place to get them out of France. By then, France was divided into the occupied and non-occupied zones, and getting through to the non-occupied zone was both difficult and dangerous. Even if the escapees did succeed, there was no guarantee of freedom.

That was when Nathalie's family became involved. One day, a message arrived for her father from Antoine saying that they were setting up escape routes throughout France with the aim of getting people out over the Pyrénées. Was he willing to stick his neck out? Èmile Fontaine consulted his wife. They were aware of the dangers involved. Already the borders were closed. Soldiers now patrolled all the exit roads to Spain and Vichy and German spies were keeping a close eye on the comings and goings in the nearby villages and towns. At first Nathalie's mother thought it unwise, even though her sympathies were with the escapees. They had four other children to think about, all younger than Nathalie. Besides, her elderly parents lived with them.

One night, in the middle of a particularly harsh winter, they heard a strange sound coming from the barn. Her father picked up a torch and his hunter's rifle, and went outside to take a look.

'Be careful,' his wife whispered. 'It could be a trap.'

The snow swirled in a thick blizzard making it difficult to see more than a few feet in front of him. He pushed the barn door open. Screeching, it swang back against the outside wall.

'Who's there? Come out or I'll shoot.'

4

A moaning sound came from behind a pile of hay. Èmile Fontaine pointed the gun in the direction and kicked a bale of hay away with his foot. Behind it was a sandy-haired youth lying in a crumpled heap on the floor.

'Help me,' he said, the words barely audible, 'I've been shot.'

Èmile ran back to the house to fetch his wife and together they carried the man into the house. Nathalie had seen it all from her bedroom window and ran downstairs to see what was happening.

'Make sure the children are in their rooms,' her mother said, as they laid him on the couch. 'I don't want them seeing this.'

Nathalie assured her parents that her siblings were all asleep. She wanted to help. The man was trying to speak, but the pain was too much and he passed out.

'He's not French,' her father said.

'I think he's English,' Nathalie replied.

Her father took off the man's coat and shirt, whilst her mother went to get a bowl of hot water and a cloth. Nathalie searched through the man's pockets, but there was nothing to identify him. The wound was from a bullet that had entered his upper chest and the blood was hard to stem.

'He will die if we don't get him to a doctor,' Èmile told them.

'We can't possibly move him,' his wife replied. 'It's impossible. And what if he dies here? Oh God, what shall we do?'

She became frantic.

'I'll fetch the doctor,' Nathalie said. 'It's the only thing we can do.'

'It's too dangerous to involve Arnaud. What if he tells the authorities?' her mother replied anxiously.

'It's a risk we're going to have to take,' Èmile said. 'We can't have his death on our hands?'

'We didn't shoot him,' her mother snapped.'

'Maman, calm down! It will be fine. We've known Arnaud for years.'

Èmile ignored his wife and looked at his daughter. 'Get going; quickly. He won't last much longer.'

Nathalie rugged up in her thick winter coat, hat and scarf, and closed the door quietly behind her in order not to disturb the rest of the household. Arnaud, the local doctor, lived a short walk away. In daylight, someone would have seen her. Thankfully no one would be out on such a night as this. Then it dawned on her. When she knocked on the door, his wife would want to know what the commotion was all about.

She rang the doorbell. A light come on in the hallway.

'Coming, coming!' a man's voice called out.

Dr Arnaud was surprised to find Nathalie standing on the doorstep.

'You have to come quickly. We need your help,' she whispered.

A voice from another room called out.

'Who is it at this time of the night?'

Nathalie stared at him with frightened eyes. 'It's my grandfather, Mme Arnaud,' she shouted out. 'He has severe chest pains and we're worried he may be having a heart attack.'

Arnaud could tell that wasn't the reason he had been called out on a night like this, nevertheless, he would go with her. Nathalie would not tell him the reason for her visit. Instead she waited until he arrived at the house and saw the man for himself.

'You won't tell anyone, will you?' her mother asked nervously. 'I mean we only just found...'

Èmile put his hand out to stop his wife from saying any more. 'Is he going to live?' he asked.

Arnaud checked the man's pulse and retrieved several instruments from his bag. 'Yes, but only if I remove this bullet straight away. Fetch me some hot water and alcohol.'

It took just over an hour to remove the bullet and stem the bleeding.

'Thankfully, it narrowly missed his heart and aorta. He's one lucky man,' said Arnaud, as he stitched the wound.

Èmile poured them all a cognac. 'Will you report him?' he asked.

Arnaud shrugged. 'My dear friend, would it surprise you to hear that he's not the first man I've helped over the past few months?'

Èmile threw a quick glance towards his wife.

'The fact that the Germans are watching the border doesn't mean people won't try to escape,' Arnaud said. 'And who can blame them? Don't worry, this is our secret. Keep the man hidden for a few days. I will come and check him. When all is well, he can be on his way and he will no longer be your problem.'

After he'd gone, the three looked at the young man lying asleep on the couch.

'Well, that's it then,' Mme Fontaine said, matter-of-factly. 'We have to play our part in this. These men need us.'

Èmile took his wife's hand and told her how much he loved her for agreeing to help.

'We must keep this between the three of us,' she replied. 'None of the children or my parents must ever get wind of our involvement, is that clear?'

Nathalie kissed her mother's cheek. 'I am proud of you, Maman.'

The next day, Èmile telephoned Paris. 'Uncle Antoine, count us in,' he said.

'Good man,' Antoine replied.

The phone went dead. One could never be sure if the wires were being tapped. The less said the better.

The Englishman remained hidden in the barn for another two weeks, returning to the house only when the children and grandparents were asleep. After one final check from Arnaud, he was considered well enough to continue his journey and left the next day with the doctor. No questions were asked.

Before long, Nathalie and her parents were helping others escape. If they thought it would just be men, they were wrong. Many were women and children.

Antoine poured out a glass of eau de vie. Knowing how much Nathalie's family were risking their own lives had made him wonder if he'd done the right thing in contacting them, yet as the occupation dragged on and things got worse for the French, he reasoned anyone could lose their life at any time, regardless of circumstances. A free France meant some must die for others to live. That was just the way it was.

CHAPTER TWO

Nathalie was still fast asleep when Mme Reynaud knocked on her door with her breakfast; a piece of baguette, a pat of butter, plum jam, a boiled egg and a cup of real coffee.

'I made the butter myself with the skin from boiled milk,' she said with a smile. 'As for other things, it pays to have a few friends around here. I give them the occasional bunch of flowers and they make sure a few things are kept aside for me. It saves us having to queue up for hours on end. Even so, rationing is hitting us all hard, but we manage.'

She put the tray on a small table by the window and went over to the stove. A few pieces of wood had been hastily shoved inside, ready to be lit. 'I'm sorry we didn't light it yesterday. We couldn't be sure when you'd arrive and we didn't want to waste the wood. Antoine will bring more up for you today.' She sat on the bed whilst Nathalie threw on some clothes.

'We didn't want to discuss everything the network does last night. You were too tired and needed to rest. I do hope you are aware of the danger you've put yourself in by coming here. What we are doing is not for the faint-hearted.'

Nathalie began to eat her breakfast and listened.

'Naturally, I cannot divulge everything,' Mme Reynaud continued. 'Your job will be to act as a courier; possibly a few other things, depending on the circumstances.'

'What other things?'

'Keeping watch whilst an operation is taking place. The odd surveillance work, etc.'

'That doesn't sound too difficult.'

'None of it *sounds* difficult, but when you can get shot or deported to Germany, simply because you happened to be in the wrong place at the wrong time, or someone takes a dislike to you, then it becomes dangerous. We also operate after curfew which means you can be shot on sight.'

'I am aware of all this,' Nathalie answered. 'We weren't immune to it at home either. After I saw my first public execution, something snapped and I was determined not to let them beat me.'

Mme Reynaud saw the steely look of determination in her eyes. 'I'm glad to hear it. Why don't you spend the day getting to know the neighbourhood? You are welcome to join us for dinner this evening.'

She picked up the tray and left the room, leaving Nathalie to mull over her words. She knew she was risking her life, yet at the same time she couldn't deny there was a frisson of excitement about being a part of something dangerous.

She looked out of the window. The rain had stopped, the sky was a cloudless pale blue, and the autumn sun was shining, casting a glorious glow on the Parisian rooftops. The Reynauds had given her an apartment at the top of the building on the fifth floor. The first floor was their own, and the others were occupied by two couples and an elderly widower who Antoine said they'd known for years and who kept very much to themselves. The building was typical of others in the area; elegant and fashionable blocks, built in the heyday during the days of Louis XIV and

Baron Haussmann. The apartment was certainly not luxurious, but it was adequate and well appointed, and she was grateful to have it. When she looked at the wood heater, with its art nouveau green and white tiles, her heart sank. The fireplace hardly seemed big enough to heat the room, and she certainly wouldn't be able to afford the luxury of a fire every day. Winter wasn't going to be easy.

Before she left the house, Antoine gave her a map and pointed out the nearby sites. After taking a stroll along the Seine towards Pont Alexandre III, she headed towards the Hotel Ritz, which she knew had been taken over by the German hierarchy. Throughout the walk, she noticed small groups of people silently huddled together, reading notices plastered on walls. She stopped to read them. They sent shivers down her spine. All were printed on red paper bordered in black, and the text was written in both German and French.

Each one pertained to one violation only: *Shot for Spying, Shot for participation in an anti-German demonstration, Five Communists guillotined,* etc. The lists were endless. Each one bothered her, but it was the last two in particular that resonated. *Henceforth, all French people arrested will be considered hostages. When a hostile act occurs, a number of hostages commensurate with the seriousness of the act will be shot.* Another stated that a reward of a million francs would be paid to anyone who denounced the perpetrator of a particular deed. In times of hardship, there were plenty of people who would sell their mothers for such a tempting sum.

She continued walking until she came to the Place Vendôme, festooned with huge red and black Nazi flags. Gleaming black cars lined up outside the Ritz. Most likely the only Frenchmen entering would have to be collaborators, and very soon they would have the French people to answer to, because of their treachery. Nathalie didn't loiter. Her drab clothing alone would attract unwanted attention. She scurried away, disgusted.

On her way back, she bought a newspaper and stopped at a

busy café with tables set out on the pavement. The cakes looked delicious and she decided to treat herself to one. With sugar rationed, she wondered how they could still make such delights. One look at the clientele answered her question. Most of them were German officers who had the money to pay for such luxuries. A sense of normalcy had to be maintained.

Natalie sipped her coffee and ate her cake, which cost her far more than she could afford, and read the newspaper. Apart from Vichy propaganda, which she glossed over, some of it centred on the Jews. Declarations were made that most of the foreign Jews had left the country of their own free will. No one could surely believe this, she told herself. Who on earth would leave all their worldly goods behind at such short notice and surrender themselves up to the people they had run away from?

Her thoughts drifted back to the last six months in the village. Her parents and Dr Arnaud had helped over a hundred Jews, and that was just their network. How many others had been fortunate to escape over the perilous mountains? Nathalie was well aware that in July 1942, the homes of at least 7,000 foreign Jews had been raided. Almost 18,000 were rounded up. A quarter of them were children. Almost all of them ended up in Poland. It was a national shame.

Later that evening over dinner, Mme Reynaud announced that they would be having visitors who she'd like her to meet.

Six people arrived that night. Five men and a young, blonde girl, Sylvie, who Nathalie surmised was not much older than herself. The men ranged between their twenties to late middle age. One of the men in particular caught her attention. Pierre was a softy spoken man in his late twenties or early thirties with dark hair and astonishingly warm, hypnotic eyes. His mouth was full and soft – almost too feminine, but sensuous all the same. But most of all, it was his face that struck her. He looked drawn and haunted. She couldn't be sure why and wanted to know more about him. A tall, balding man, who introduced himself as Paul, took charge of the meeting. With his wire-rimmed glasses and grey goatee beard, he reminded Nathalie of a science professor.

After welcoming her to Paris, Paul set about outlining the things they needed to discuss. The most important topic that night was the twelve Jews who were being hidden in a church crypt by a Priest. Over the past few days, there had been intensive searches in the area and the priest feared that it would only be a day or two at the most, before the church came under further scrutiny.

As the evening wore on, Nathalie learnt that one of their main escape routes was via the coal barges that plied the Seine. The barges stopped at various pick-up and drop-off points all the way down through the canal systems until they reached the river Yonne. From there, the escapees took a circuitous overland route towards the Pyrénées. She recalled that none of the people her parents helped had ever mentioned how they got there for fear of the information getting into the wrong hands.

'There will be a barge arriving tomorrow,' Paul said. 'We're going to have to move our "package" out quickly.'

The plan was to get the Jewish escapees from the crypt and into the Paris underground sewer system, where they would exit next to the Pont de l'Alma, a stone's throw away from the house, and near the Seine. It was to take place after midnight.

'Are you up for it, Nathalie?' Paul asked.

Everyone looked at her, waiting for her reply. This was it, she thought to herself, as his words sank in. It wasn't a game. This was the real thing.

'Certainly,' she replied.

'Good girl.' Paul turned to Sylvie. 'The two of you will work together. You know the ropes.'

Sylvie nodded in agreement. She was to pick Nathalie up from *La Vie en Fleurs*, and they would meet him at the specific place near the entrance to the sewers at the Pont de l'Alma.

After more discussions about safe houses and a cache of guns that had recently been acquired, the group dispersed. Nathalie also took her leave. Antoine had lit the fire in her room and she sat in front of it for a while thinking about the events that were to take place. In no time at all she was fast asleep.

.

CHAPTER THREE

An hour before curfew, Sylvie and Nathalie left 29 rue Frédéric Chopin for the rendezvous point. The Reynauds had already left. A combination of the blackout and low clouds blocking out the moon, meant that it was pitch dark. They could hardly see their own shadows. Sylvie warned her that although this was good for them, the Germans would be particularly alert, and they must not let their guard down.

She was right. They had only just left rue Frédéric Chopin when they heard the sound of an engine coming towards them. Sylvie grabbed Nathalie's arm and pulled her into a doorway only seconds before a truck passed by, shining its searchlights into the street. The pair pressed themselves hard against the inside of a doorway and held their breath. The bright light swung in their direction as it passed, lighting up the doorway and barely missing them by a few inches. When the truck turned out of the street, they leapt out of the shadows and hurried towards the quay in the direction of the bridge. There they saw another truck driving slowly backwards and forth across the bridge, casting it's searchlights up and down the river.

'What did I tell you,' Sylvie whispered. 'They are not so silly that they don't recognise we operate under the cloak of darkness.'

Inching their way along the quayside via the recesses of doorways that opened out onto the street, they managed to make their way to the entrance of the sewers. The entrance was via a set of steps partially hidden from view by bushes. At the bottom of the steps was a padlocked door. The sewers were out of bounds and patrols regularly checked all the entrances. Anyone caught trying to get in or out would be shot on sight.

To Nathalie, it seemed an impossible task. How could anyone get in or out, or even hang about in the area without being spotted? What she hadn't reckoned was that the house opposite, the same building whose doorway they now stood in, belonged to a résistance member. When the door opened, her heart missed a beat. The house belonged to Paul.

'*Mon Dieu*! You gave me a fright,' she said in a hushed voice.

Paul put a forefinger to his lips. 'Shush!!!'

He ushered them inside, leaving the door slightly ajar, and they stood in the shadows, waiting. After a few minutes, another man entered. Pierre.

'Just in time,' Paul whispered.

Pierre checked his watch. They waited a few more minutes, and then he stepped back outside again, saying he would give them a signal when he was ready.

The trio watched through the crack of the door as Pierre ran across the road and disappeared down the steps. Nathalie counted the minutes. After what seemed like an interminable amount of time, two lights flashed through the bushes.

'He's done it,' Paul said, breathing a sigh of relief. 'Right, come on. Let's get them out before the patrols are back.'

They hurried across the road and down the steps just in time to help Pierre pull away the chains and padlocks and wrench open the door. Tired, wet, and dirty from slipping through the sewers, the Jews were clamouring on the other side to get out. The ghastly drawn looks etched on their faces, made them look eerily like supernatural beings being disgorged from the bowels of the earth. Nathalie was both shocked and deeply moved by their plight, especially when she saw an elderly couple and two small children with them.

Two résistants were with them, one of whom she'd met the other night. The men ushered them up the steps and into the bushes. Paul told Nathalie to take care of the little ones whilst he and Sylvie helped the elderly couple. When everyone was out, Pierre gave the signal to move on whilst he stayed behind to put the padlocks and chains back in place. It was imperative that the door looked as though it had not been touched.

Nathalie took the two children by their hands and told them not to be frightened. The look in their eyes made her want to weep. In all her life, she had never seen children with such fear. The group began to file through the bushes towards the Pont de l'Alma. She looked back to see if Pierre was following. He was nowhere in sight.

At a point where the bridge started to cross the Seine, Paul held up the flat of his hand and cautioned them to stop. This was the most dangerous part. The spotlights on the bridge had to be timed to see how long they would have before they could cross the road and descend the steep, slippery steps that led to a long, loading pier, part of which disappeared under the bridge. It was so dark that even with the soft reflection on the water, Nathalie could not see the barge that would carry the Jews to safety. One of the children started to whimper. She knelt down and whispered words of comfort as she wrapped her arms around them.

A signal was soon given and the group headed for the pier in pairs, each one waiting until the searchlights had passed. She was the last to leave with the children. When she clasped their tiny hands tighter, telling them that this was a little game they were playing, she heard a rustling sound in the bushes. Pierre re-appeared, and without saying a word, scooped up one of the children in his arms and headed across the road.

'Quickly,' he hissed.

Within minutes they were gathered under the bridge and Nathalie breathed a sigh of relief when she saw the dark shape of a coal barge waiting for them. Safe in the knowledge that the searchlights could not reach them, the captain, aided by one of his associates, helped the escapees embark. After the last person boarded, Paul checked that they were safely stowed away in the hiding place under the deck. A flashlight was given to them along with bedding, food and water, and a makeshift container to be used as a toilet. After satisfying himself all was well, the planks were secured in place, and coal sacks were carefully placed on top to prevent the hiding place being discovered during inspections. If all went well, the escapees would stay cooped up in these cramped dark conditions for the next few days. After that, their journey for freedom would take another circuitous route, and it was unlikely whether Nathalie or any of her friends would know whether their escape had been successful.

Paul handed the captain a wad of money and they shook hands. His was a highly dangerous job and should the Jews be found, he had nowhere to turn. Death would be swift.

Nathalie was too exhilarated to sleep that night, and lay in bed going over and over the events of the previous few hours in her mind. At home, she had known what was taking place in her village, but rarely came into contact with the people her parents were trying to help. The Englishman was an exception. Her role had been little more than keeping watch whilst others took the risks. Now, she couldn't get the terrified look on the escapees' faces out of her mind. How could her country be a part of all this? The thought sickened her.

The next morning, the Reynauds were back in the shop. Antoine was setting up a display of pink and white cyclamens in the window and Madeleine was cutting the stems from a bunch of roses to make bouquets.

'It went well last night,' she said. 'From what I hear, you were a natural with the children.'

Nathalie told her their plight had only strengthened her resolve to do more. She asked how many times the group had done that sort of thing.

'More than I can count,' Mme Reynaud replied. 'It started with soldiers after Dunkerque; first one, then another. We never expected our country to turn on the Jews though. That's when we began to hide them in small groups. It's not so difficult to hide one or two people, but a whole family, well that's something else. After the round-ups, the numbers swelled. And there are also political dissidents who have a price on their head. We had to turn to the church for help; even the mosques.

'Antoine and I were at the church last night. We were helping to get the group into the sewers. The opening wasn't through a door like the one at Pont de l'Alma. It was down a manhole. Can you imagine the distress that caused?'

'Have you ever lost anyone?' Nathalie asked. 'Those sewers are dangerous. It's easy to slip when you only have a flashlight to guide you.'

Mme Reynaud sighed. 'One evening we lost a whole group. There were ten of them. The last two were preparing to enter the sewer when the Germans turned up and opened fire. They were killed as was one of our own men. Another fled. Of course the rest of the escapees heard the screams and gunshots and started to panic. Our men urged them on, but the Germans wasted no time in going down after them. In the ensuing chaos, they were not fast enough and were gunned down. Another of our men was also killed there. Only two escaped. It didn't end there. The Gestapo pounced, raiding every building in the area. At least fifty innocent men and women were detained and not all made it home. That's what we are up against.'

Antoine finished his flower display and made them all a hot drink. He looked tired. Madeleine told him to go and have a lie down. Nathalie offered to help out in the shop in gratitude for them giving her the apartment.

'I could do with the help,' Madeleine replied, 'although I can't afford to pay you very much. It may be better if you try to find yourself another job.'

Nathalie had a little money put aside but she knew it wouldn't last long. For the moment, she was content to help the Reynauds. It would also give everyone in the neighbourhood a chance to familiarize themselves with her. A stranger in their midst could provoke too many questions.

CHAPTER FOUR

Over the next few weeks, Nathalie learnt the finer points of working as a florist. The correct way to cut flowers, what to add to the water to preserve them, which flowers were in season, and choosing the right flowers for floral arrangements and bouquets. It was work that she had never expected to do but she took to it with enthusiasm and creativity, especially when it came to gift-wrapping, which due to the diminishing lack of coloured papers and ribbons, stretched her imagination to the limits.

The art of floristry was not the only work that Nathalie did. It gave her a cover to pass messages. Mme Reynaud would arrange a special bouquet, and Nathalie would deliver it, along with a coded message. After a few months, she knew the area from the 8th Arrondissement to the 16th, like the back of her hand.

During the following months, she participated in several more escapes, most of which took place in other areas along the Seine. So far, all of them had gone well, but it worried her that this run of luck wouldn't last. One day in February 1943, she was asked to deliver a bouquet to Pierre. She had only seen him once since the night of the first escape at the Pont de l'Alma.

It was mid-afternoon when Nathalie left rue Frédéric Chopin, and the weather was particularly bad. A combination of sleet and snow and below zero temperatures meant walking was hazardous. Rugged up in her thick coat, she took the Metro from Alma-Marceau to Abbesses. The entrance to the Metro, with its green Art Nouveau, vine-like wrought-iron arches and amber lights, was one of the most beautiful in Paris, but Nathalie was far too cold to think of sight-seeing. She headed up the hill towards the Place du Tertre and the Basilica of Sacré Cœur where she was told Pierre lived in an apartment above a bistro.

The ice glistened on the cobblestones and although she was careful, she slipped, falling heavily on her back. A searing pain in her ankle caused her to cry out loud. *Damn*, she thought to herself. *That's all I need.* She stood up, wincing at the pain, and brushed the slush from her coat. When she saw the flowers that Mme Reynaud had so carefully put together, her heart sank. Hardly a flower head was intact. She stooped to pick them up and was conscious of a black Citroen stationed at the end of the road with its engine idling. The driver put the car into gear and slowly drove towards her. It pulled up by the side of the pavement and the passenger got out.

'Can I help?' he asked. 'You appear to have had an accident. Are you alright?'

He spoke French with a German accent and he wore a smart, calf-length leather coat over a dark suit. She glanced at the driver but could barely make out his face under the fedora. Nathalie's heart skipped a beat. The Gestapo.

'I'm fine, thank you,' she stammered. 'It was just a light fall; nothing serious.'

The man took off one of his gloves, and proceeded to flick more slush from the back of her coat.

'That's better.' He took one look at the bouquet and frowned, 'which is more than can be said for these. Do you live locally?'

His manner unnerved her. He was polite, yet there was no smile or warmth on his face. She prayed that he wouldn't press her for the address.

'I'm visiting an aunt. She's been rather ill just lately. The flowers are for her.'

The man put his glove back on. 'May we offer you a lift?'

Nathalie's heart pounded in her chest. 'I'm fine, really, I am. She only lives two blocks away.'

'As you wish, Mademoiselle.'

He got back into the car and drove away leaving Nathalie quivering with fright on the pavement. When they turned the corner, she breathed a sigh of relief. They hadn't even asked her name or checked her identity papers.

Pierre lived in a street off the Place du Tertre. He was looking out the window when she arrived, as if he was waiting for her. Moments later, a door next to the bistro opened and he ushered her up a narrow flight of steps to his apartment

'You're late,' he said, 'and you're limping. Are you alright?'

'I slipped. Unfortunately I destroyed Mme Reynaud's beautiful bouquet in the process. I'm sorry.'

He took the flowers from her and looked at them closely.

'There's no message with them,' she added, 'just the flowers.'

'I don't need another message,' he said with a smile. 'I have everything I need here.'

His response told her something she'd suspected for a while; that the Reynauds often hid their messages in their floral arrangements. It was all about the colours and the arrangement. In this case, pink ranunculus and purple anemones with juniper and wax flowers. Nathalie had no idea what the arrangement meant, which was probably the safest thing, given her earlier encounter with the Gestapo.

She stepped inside the apartment and was pleasantly surprised. Pierre was a painter and the place was filled with his work and artist's equipment. It smelt of turpentine and oils. Every surface was covered with sketches or works in progress, paint – either in tubes or powder form, and brushes. She looked at an unfinished painting of a still life on the easel.

'Are you going to paint these?' she laughed, referring to Madeleine's flowers.

He put them in a vase and stood them on a small table. 'Flowers are not really my speciality. I prefer portraits or street scenes. It's why I live here. That's what the customers want.'

Nathalie studied the painting closely. The vividly coloured oranges, intensely yellow lemons and green apples on a white platter, placed in front of a vase of nasturtiums and convolvulus, reminded her of a Cézanne.

'It's very good. I particularly love the way you've used the brush strokes to give the fruit depth. And the white platter makes the colours sing.'

Pierre smiled at her description. 'Do you paint?' he asked.

'It might surprise you to know that I did consider becoming a painter once – before the war. Now a career of any sort is on hold; maybe after the war.' She cast a quick glance at several other paintings. 'I'm not as good as you, and I'm quite sure I wouldn't be able to make a living from it.'

When she moved away from the easel, he saw her grimace in pain.

'Take off your coat and sit down,' he said, moving aside a pile of sketches from the sofa.

'I'd better take a look at your leg.'

Pierre sat on a stool in front of her, gently pulled her boot off, and put her foot on his lap, telling her to wiggle her toes.

'The ankle is definitely swollen, but it's not broken.' He massaged it with his fingertips in a small circular motion.

Nathalie lay back against a cushion, closed her eyes and purred like a cat. 'You have no idea how good that feels. You're not only a talented artist, you have a magic touch as well.'

There was something about Pierre that Nathalie was attracted to. It wasn't just his dark, brooding looks; he was sensitive and she felt at ease in his company, as if all her fears were falling away and life was as it used to be before the war.

'Where did you study?' she asked, her eyes still closed.

'Here in Paris, at the École des Beaux-Arts.'

'Then you're in good company. I believe Degas, Ingres and Renoir studied there also.' She sat forward whilst he continued to massage her lower leg. 'And if you don't think me too impolite, do you still manage to earn a living now that the war is on?'

'I'm not rich if that's what you mean,' he replied. 'But I manage. Montmartre is still a tourist spot, you know, even if the clientele has changed.'

'You mean the Germans?'

'Of course; they love to sightsee around here. For some reason, it makes them think they're on holiday and not at war.'

'And they actually pay you for your work?'

'Perhaps I've been lucky. Only the odd one or two have wanted to cheat me. Many come here with their Parisian girlfriends and want to impress. Sometimes it's those same women – horizontal collaborators – who make them pay the asking price. Funny how human nature works isn't it?' He put her leg down and asked if she'd like a drink. 'I only have red wine,' he said. 'Not a very good one, I'm afraid.'

'You paint a rosier picture than I'd imagined,' Nathalie replied. 'I saw the Gestapo on my way here, and they weren't sightseeing. In fact I would say they were definitely staking the area out – like bloodhounds.'

Pierre took a sip of his wine. 'We're used to each other.'

Nathalie thought that an odd comment. How could anyone get used to the Gestapo?

'This is a Bohemian area,' he continued. 'The Gestapo think we're all communists and socialists. They raid us frequently.'

'Have you ever been raided?'

'Yes, once. They ransacked the place and left. I think it was a warning.'

'I didn't think the Gestapo did warnings,' she replied, dryly.

Pierre finished his wine. 'Would you care for a bite to eat before you return? I don't have much here. I usually eat in the bistro downstairs.'

Nathalie accepted. The more she was in his company, the more he intrigued her.

It was late afternoon and the bistro was almost empty. The owner, Jean, was a rotund man with a ruddy complexion, and he welcomed Pierre with the familiarity of a family member. As food was rationed, a menu was not offered.

'I'll have whatever the chef recommends,' Pierre said tactfully.

'In which case, we have a hearty bean stew cooked in beef stock,' Jean replied. 'And Mademoiselle?'

'The same, thank you,' said Nathalie.

Pierre told her that the bistro had been in the same family since the end of the nineteenth century. 'They have a reputation of being loyal to artists. When we can't pay, we offer them a painting which they hang on the walls. If it sells, they pay us and we pay our bill. If it doesn't, they keep the painting.'

Nathalie looked at the variety of paintings adorning the walls. They ranged from small, six inch sketches and watercolours, to one that was over three feet square. Some were framed, many unframed. It resembled a small gallery.

'And are any of these yours?' she asked.

He laughed. 'Not today; maybe tomorrow.'

Nathalie thought it a very insecure life, but she was in no position to judge others when she didn't even have a job herself.

The owner placed a basket of bread and two steaming bowls of soup in front of them. It was accompanied by a carafe of red wine.

Pierre asked what brought her to Paris and she told him her story.

'And you?' she asked. 'What made you get mixed up in all this?'

'It wasn't difficult. I was ashamed when our government surrendered without a fight. At first I voiced my protest by writing messages on walls. After a short time, it was evident that anyone with libertarian views would be silenced. I don't subscribe to any doctrine except freedom, but I have friends who are committed communists. Some of them were hauled away and badly beaten, others have disappeared completely. What am I to do? I cannot be an onlooker to such things.'

Nathalie understood his sentiments, but it was what he said after this that shocked her.

'And then there was Anna.'

'Who's Anna?' she asked.

'She was my lover. We studied together.'

Nathalie blushed with embarrassment. 'I'm sorry. I didn't mean to pry.'

Pierre continued. 'She was my lover and she was Jewish. Her family came here from Berlin in 1933.'

Nathalie felt uncomfortable. 'Please, Pierre, you don't have to say any more.'

He looked into her eyes. 'I want to talk about her. I've bottled it up for too long. At first the government promised no harm would come to any Jew, and then, at the end of 1940, her father was dismissed from his post at the university. It spiralled downwards after that. Their identity cards were marked "Jew", they were not allowed in cafés or any public space such as gardens, and could only travel in the last compartment on the metro. They even had separate curfew hours which meant that they missed out on food and starved.'

Pierre's face took on the same haunted look he wore the first time she met him.

'You cannot possibly have known what it was like here, Nathalie. In June of the following year, they were all forced to wear the yellow star. If it wasn't sewn on accurately, they were beaten.'

He went on to tell her of more restrictions.

'I knew it was bad,' she said, 'but until now, I never really understood just how bad. It's hard to comprehend.'

'Some of them escaped to the Free Zone. They were the lucky ones. I urged Anna's family to flee, but they wouldn't hear of it. At the end of July, the round-ups started. Anna's family were in bed when the police burst into their home at three-o'clock in the morning and ordered them to prepare a suitcase and accompany them outside to a waiting truck. By now, her parents were worn down, and coming from Germany, they did have an idea of what might happen. Against her wishes, her parents told her to escape out of the window onto a narrow ledge which led to the back garden. She hid there, listening to the screaming and shouts until it was all quiet. The next day, she arrived at my apartment.'

'Did anyone here know she was Jewish?' Nathalie asked. 'I mean...' she inclined her head towards Jean.

'The subject of religion wasn't brought up, but there were colleagues at the art school who knew her background.'

'Wasn't it dangerous to hide her?'

Pierre sighed. 'I would have done anything for her. It was natural to hide her.'

Nathalie hated herself for asking such a question.

'That's when we decided to actively join a Résistance group. Of course, it wasn't easy. They didn't exactly advertise for recruits! But I knew Paul and that helped. When he realized we were genuine, he introduced us to the Reynauds who had created an escape network for British servicemen. They put us through quite a few tests before they were sure of our commitment. Because of Anna, we came into contact with other Jews in hiding and our escape network expanded. Soon we were aiding all sorts of people. It wasn't only Jews, but political dissidents and homosexuals. Then one night, an escape went wrong.'

Nathalie felt a lump rise in her throat. She had a sickening feeling she knew what was coming next.

'We had almost finished getting the last escapees into the sewers when the Germans arrived.' Pierre became agitated. He ran his hands through his hair and rubbed his temples with his fingers. 'It was a bloodbath. They killed all the escapees and some of our own. I was at the Pont de l'Alma with Paul. We knew something had gone wrong when no-one arrived. The next day, I discovered Anna was one of those killed.'

'You weren't responsible,' Nathalie said, trying to offer a little comfort. 'It can happen to any of us at any time?'

'I shouldn't have let her go there. That part of the escape is very dangerous. Trying to get people into a dark manhole scares the hell out of them.'

'Mme Reynaud told me about that escape, but she never said who was killed. Apparently only one man managed to escape when the Germans turned up. Do you know who it was?'

'Gilbert. We call him "the Communist" because of his radical Marxist leanings.'

'Wasn't Gilbert one of the men at the Reynauds the night I first met you?' Nathalie asked, 'a rather quiet man with light brown hair and a short beard.'

'That's him. He assists with false IDs and distributes leaflets.'

By the time they'd finished their meal, it was dark and Nathalie said she'd better be getting back. Pierre offered to walk her to the Metro but she wouldn't hear of it. As much as she wanted to stay longer in his company, she was afraid the Gestapo might still be hanging around.

'Thank Mme Reynaud for the flowers,' he said. 'Tell her that I approved of her choice of colours.'

They shook hands and Nathalie headed back down the hill, wondering if his words, *I approved of her choice of colours*, was also a coded message.

CHAPTER FIVE

The following week, Nathalie and Mme Reynaud were arranging flowers in the shop when Pierre unexpectedly paid them a visit.

'I happened to be in the area and thought I'd call by to give you this,' he said, handing Nathalie a flat parcel wrapped in newspaper.

When she opened it, she was surprised to find it was the still life he'd been working on.

'You expressed your delight with it and I would like you to have it. I also wondered if you'd care to join me later this afternoon. There's a cinema not far from here and they happen to be showing one of my favourite films – *Les Enfants du Paradis*. That is if Mme Reynaud can spare you for a while.'

Mme Reynaud smiled when she saw Nathalie's face light up. She was a woman of the world and had recognized her attraction to him the first time she laid eyes on him.

'It will do you good to get away for a while,' she said. 'Go and enjoy yourself.'

'Then it's settled,' Pierre said. 'I will pick you up in an hour.'

When he'd gone, Nathalie confided in Mme Reynaud that Pierre had told her about Anna.

'What was she like?' she asked.

Mme Reynaud picked up a few flowers and started to cut the stems, deliberating over her response. 'She was a beautiful girl and her death touched us all, but if we are to do our work successfully, we cannot dwell on the past. Now, if you'll pass me those flowers, I'll continue here, and you go and pretty yourself up.'

Her sharp reply told Nathalie the subject was closed.

By the time Pierre returned, Nathalie had transformed herself. The decision about what to wear wasn't a difficult one. She had only brought two good outfits for special occasions; one for winter, the other for summer. As it was still winter, she wore a pencil-slim, charcoal grey skirt with a figure-hugging, cream jumper which complimented her shoulder-length dark hair. After applying a little rouge and red lipstick, she studied herself in the mirror. Something was missing. The outfit needed a pretty scarf or a piece of jewellery. She remembered the string of pearls her mother had given her as a farewell present. As pretty as she looked, she would still have to wear her drab, thick winter coat, and after her fall, it was in desperate need of a good clean. It would have to do.

Les Enfants du Paradis always guaranteed a good audience and the cinema was packed. It had been a few years since Nathalie had seen a film; the war had changed everything. All the little things she took for granted had gone, replaced by survival and a deep suspicion of everyone and everything. She stole a glance at Pierre as they watched the film. His presence made her realise there was a life out there to be enjoyed.

He caught her looking at him. 'What are you thinking?' he asked, with a smile.

'I'd almost forgotten what it was like to have a normal life.'

He reached for her hand. 'So had I,' he said in a soft whisper.

Nathalie felt a warm glow radiate through her body. His words and touch gave her goosebumps. Where it would lead, she had no idea. For the moment, she was happy just to be near him.

After the film, they took a stroll along the Seine eventually stopping at a bar for a drink.

'I was most impressed with the way you unlocked the chains and the sewer door at the Pont de l'Alma entrance,' Nathalie said. 'Where did you learn to do that?'

Pierre laughed. 'It's a skill I picked up from an escapologist a while back'

Nathalie's eyes widened. 'You mean a magician?'

'A magician, yes, although he managed to make a very good living from escapology – travelling circuses and side shows; that kind of thing. He lived in Montmartre for a while and we became friends. That's when he taught me some of the tricks of his trade. At the time, I didn't know I would ever put them to use.'

'Where is he now?'

'I have no idea, but knowing him, I imagine he's using his skills in the same way that I am.'

'And are all your friends as colourful?'

Pierre laughed. 'Perhaps. Being colourful isn't such a bad thing, especially in times like this.'

Nathalie's face betrayed more than a hint of concern. 'Not unless it attracts the attention of the wrong people.'

Pierre changed the subject. 'I was wondering if you would care to sit for me one day. It would give me great pleasure to paint your portrait.'

'I'd be honoured,' she replied, thrilled that he should consider her worth painting at all.

'Good. Then let's say in a week's time. And wear those pearls,' he added. 'They suit you.'

It was past closing time when Nathalie returned and *La Vie en Fleurs* was still open. As she neared the shop, she could see the Reynauds through the window. They had a visitor. At the sound of the door opening, the man spun around. It was Gilbert.

'Ahh, if it isn't the delightful Mademoiselle Fontaine. Madame Reynaud told me you went to the cinema. Did you enjoy the film?'

'It was a most pleasant afternoon, thank you,' Nathalie replied, taking off her hat and coat.

Gilbert cast a quick eye over her. 'May I say how particularly attractive you look this evening.'

She had no idea if the Reynauds had told him she'd gone out with Pierre and she didn't offer to tell him. Mme Reynaud asked her if she'd be so kind as to go outside and bring the flowers in. Outside, Nathalie caught a glimpse of the three of them through the window as she picked up a large bucket of roses. Even though she'd left the door ajar, it was impossible to hear what they were saying. Then she noticed Gilbert pull out a small package from the inside pocket of his overcoat and place it on the counter. Mme Reynaud quickly slid it under the counter. They shook hands and Antoine walked him to the door. Gilbert doffed his hat towards Nathalie as he left.

'Good night, Mademoiselle Fontaine. It was a pleasure to see you again.'

The next morning, the Reynauds asked Nathalie if she'd mind looking after the shop as they had urgent business to attend to. They had only just left when she heard the roar of trucks pulling up in the street. Within minutes, the street was blocked off and soldiers carrying machine guns began a search of all the houses. Nathalie was serving an elderly woman at the time, and the woman almost passed out in fear. In that instant, the package Gilbert gave to Mme Reynaud flashed through her mind. She remembered seeing her hide it under the counter and took a quick look to see if it was still there. It was hidden under a few sheets of wrapping paper, well out of sight. Instinct made her pick it up and drop it into an empty bucket. She quickly grabbed a large container of roses and placed it on top. Fortunately, her customer was too pre-occupied with the unfolding situation taking place in the street to notice what she was doing. She placed the bucket outside the door, where it blended in with the rest of the display. Seconds later, she faced the barrel of a gun.

'Your papers,' the man asked. 'Quickly.'

Nathalie ran back inside and took them out of her bag. By now the man was accompanied by half a dozen others, all carrying guns. He indicated to them to search the premises whilst he scrutinized her papers.

'Who else lives here?' he asked.

'Just the owners: Madame and Monsieur Reynaud.'

'Where are they?'

Nathalie thought quickly. 'Monsieur Reynaud is at the flower market and Madame is making a floral delivery.' Nathalie was aware of several Germans living in the area as she'd made deliveries to their apartments herself. She tried to recall a name to throw them off. 'Rue Napoleon, I believe. Herr Schubert regularly orders flowers. Sometimes roses, other times...'

'Enough!' the man shouted.

He turned his attention to the old woman. By this time she was in tears and her hands shook visibly when she handed him her papers. He examined them, threw them back at her and started to look around the shop. Nathalie watched helplessly whilst he ransacked drawers and glass cabinets, at one point knocking over a Lalique vase which shattered at her feet. Upstairs she could hear the sound of heavy footsteps as the men searched the rest of the building. Ten minutes later they returned, saying that all was in order. The man took one last look at Nathalie and they left. She breathed a deep sigh of relief and ran to comfort the elderly woman who was clutching her chest with severe pains.

From the safety of the shop window, they watched soldiers march frightened groups of men and women towards the trucks at gunpoint. Guard dogs strained at their leashes, barking and jumping around them, their handlers taking obvious delight in frightening the hapless prisoners. To Nathalie it seemed as if they were in the area for an eternity. In reality it was barely half an hour.

The Reynauds, returning home when rue Frédéric Chopin was blocked off, witnessed the events from the other side of the blockade. When they eventually reached the shop, the first thing Mme Reynaud did was to look under the counter.

'Mon Dieu,' she cried out loud when she saw the package had disappeared. 'The identity cards have gone. We're finished!'

Nathalie lifted the roses out of the bucket to retrieve the package.

'Is this what you were looking for?' she asked.

Mme Reynaud clapped her hands together in relief. 'How on earth did you know about it?' she asked.

'I saw you put it there last night. I had no idea what was in it, but I knew you wouldn't want it ending up at Avenue Foch.'

The Reynauds applauded her quick thinking. 'We should have said something. You could have been implicated yourself,' Antoine said.

'Do you have any idea why the Germans would raid us?' Nathalie asked.

Mme Reynaud shrugged her shoulders. 'They raided the whole street which means they weren't directing their attentions on us.'

Nathalie wasn't so sure. The fact that this took place soon after Gilbert dropped the package off, caused her great concern, but she reasoned if the Gestapo knew the forged identity cards were there, they wouldn't have arrived twelve hours later. A call the same night would have been more their style.

CHAPTER SIX

Pierre added the final touches to Nathalie's portrait and took a step back to admire his handiwork.

'Finished,' he said, putting his palette and brushes down and wiping his hands. 'Anymore and I will overwork it.'

Nathalie was relieved. She'd sat in the same position for over an hour and her back was beginning to ache.

'It's wonderful,' she said, taking a closer look. 'I particularly like the way you've captured the light on my hair.'

'And the pearls,' he added. 'I like the contrast.'

'Do you think you'll be able to sell it?'

'It's not for sale.'

'But you need the money? Surely a painting such as this would pay the rent for a few weeks?'

'You may be right. All the same my mind is made up.'

Over the past few weeks, Nathalie's feelings for him had deepened. A part of her hoped he didn't want to sell the painting because she meant something to him, yet apart from the odd touch, he'd never expressed any desire for her. In fact, he'd never even attempted to kiss her. She wondered how many times he'd painted Anna. There was nothing in his studio that conjured the likeness of his ill-fated lover. Perhaps he'd sold them rather than be reminded of her.

She looked at her watch. It was time to leave and he offered to walk her to the station. It was a beautiful evening. Spring had arrived at last and Parisians strolled with a bounce in their step that not even the Germans could dispel. The sombre grey skies were now replaced with soft blues, the days getting longer, and the trees in full blossom. However, the joy Nathalie felt in Pierre's company was quickly dispelled when he told her he would be leaving Paris for a while.

Her heart sank. 'Where to?' she asked.

'I can't say.'

She found herself blushing. 'I'm sorry. That was impolite of me. It's just that, well... it's just that I've enjoyed the last few weeks. I'll miss you.'

He took her hand. 'I'll miss you too,' he replied. 'I've grown fond of you.'

Fond! Nathalie couldn't help feeling a great sense of disappointment. Was that all she meant to him? She pulled her hand away and asked for a cigarette.

'How long will you be away?' she asked as he lit her cigarette.

'I'm not sure, maybe a few weeks. It depends.'

Depends on what, Nathalie asked herself? Was he going away on an assignment? Whatever it was, he wasn't going to tell her. She quickly pulled herself together. When they reached the station, she gave him a peck on the cheek and wished him a safe trip. What had started out as an evening filled with joy had turned into a great disappointment. What a fool she'd been to allow herself to fall for him.

Pierre had only been gone a week when the group met to discuss another assignment. Paul announced that there was to be another escape at the Pont de l'Alma in three days. They would receive the all clear the afternoon it was to take place.

'It will be the last from this spot for a while,' Paul said. 'We don't want to push our luck.'

He noticed a worried look on Nathalie's face and asked what was wrong.

'I'm wondering who will take Pierre's place. He's so skilled with those locks.'

Gilbert answered. 'You don't have to worry. He's not the only one who can pick locks. I will do it.'

His eyes seemed to tell her that he knew she disliked him. Paul continued. He told her she was to make her own way to the rendezvous point as Sylvie would be helping the escapees leave the safe house.

The conversation turned to new identity cards. Gilbert would have more ready in a few days. This time they would include counterfeit baptism certificates. The Germans were asking anyone suspicious to provide them as further proof of being a Christian. Finding a priest willing to go along with the plan hadn't been easy. Church registers were regularly checked and compared against the IDs. Fortunately there were some men of the cloth who had volunteered to take the risk.

After the meeting, Mme Reynaud thought Nathalie unusually distracted.

'Is anything wrong?' she asked. 'You seem on edge.'

'I'm just worried about those locks at the Pont de l'Alma. Apart from the door itself, there are at least ten others on the actual chains. Pierre unlocked them in no time. Does Gilbert have those same skills?'

'We've all learnt to share our skills, Nathalie. Did Pierre tell you he was the only one who could do that sort of thing?'

Nathalie looked embarrassed. 'No, he didn't.'

'There you are then. Stop worrying. You'll make us all nervous.'

'I know I shouldn't ask, but do you know where Pierre has gone?'

Mme Reynaud sighed. 'Sit down. There's something you should know.'

Nathalie felt a lump rise in her throat. She should have left well alone.

'I know you have taken rather a shine to him, but the truth is, he hasn't gone away on a clandestine mission – not this time anyway. His father was pulled up in a raid and taken away. It happened just before you arrived. Now his mother is seriously ill. '

Nathalie's jaw dropped. 'What happened to his father?' she asked. 'Did they kill him?'

'No. They released him a few days later, but he was beaten so badly, he's unable to walk. His mother is ill because of it. Haven't you noticed that he sometimes looks pale and drawn? He's a private man and doesn't like to talk about it.'

'He has certainly suffered,' Nathalie replied. 'First Anna, then his father; none of us are safe.'

'This is what our life has become,' sighed Mme Reynaud. 'We live in fear, never knowing what will strike next.'

'I would like to learn how to use a gun,' Nathalie said, after a while.

This time it was Mme Reynaud's turn to look surprised. 'We deliberately avoid giving the female couriers guns in case anyone is picked up. It would mean instant imprisonment and most likely torture. Only the men keep small firearms.'

'Does Antoine have one?'

Mme Reynaud could see Nathalie wasn't going to give up. She called out to Antoine who was in another room. 'Antoine, can you please bring your pistol?'

He returned carrying a Modele 1935A semi-automatic. 'What's all this about?' he asked.

'Nathalie would like to learn how to shoot? I've already told her we don't like our female couriers carrying them.'

Antoine handed it to her. She took it cautiously.

'Do you think you could kill someone?' he asked, watching her reaction.

'I would hope not, but our work is dangerous and should the occasion occur, I'd like to be prepared.'

'Nathalie is quite right,' Antoine said to his wife. 'There's no reason why she shouldn't learn if she wants to. I've never held with the policy of only arming the men. Who knows what the future will bring.'

He explained the features of his gun, telling her how it was used by the French military until the Germans took over the factory in Alsace in 1940. Then he proceeded to dismantle it and showed her how it worked.

'Can you get me one?' Nathalie asked.

'I'll ask Paul. He is the one who handles the guns. Up to now, we have been giving them to the Maquis. The rest are stored away until the time we are called upon to liberate Paris.'

He saw the look of disappointment on her face and gave her a reassuring smile.

'Okay, I'll do my best, although what your father would say if he knew what I was doing, I dread to think.'

CHAPTER SEVEN

N athalie went through everything over and over again in her head, but she couldn't rid herself of the deep sense of unease in the pit of the stomach. At the stroke of midnight, she left the house with the Reynauds. They headed towards the Seine where they parted. Nathalie walked to Paul's house alone. As always, the escape was calculated to take place in the first phase of the lunar month when the moon was least bright. Tonight was one of those nights. Except for the bridge itself, there appeared to be no trucks with searchlights in the area.

She was within sight of Paul's house when she heard footsteps behind her. She swung around to look but there was no one in sight. She hurried on and at a point, several houses before Paul's, slipped into the recess of a large doorway and hid in the shadows. The footsteps drew nearer and suddenly stopped near the doorway. Nathalie's heart thudded loudly in her breast. It was at times like this that she wished she had a gun.

After a few seconds, the footsteps continued. She waited until they'd faded away and then peeked into the street. It was empty. Gaining her composure, she stepped back into the street and hurried to Paul's. The door was ajar. She knocked softly and pushed it open,

'You're late,' said Paul, stepping out of the shadows.

'I'm sorry, I was being cautious, I thought...' She stopped mid-sentence.

A second person stepped out of the shadows. Gilbert.

Before Nathalie could say more, Paul turned to Gilbert and told him to get a move on.

'Don't forget to signal when you're ready,' he added.

Several minutes passed and Nathalie could see Paul was becoming anxious.

'What in God's name is he doing?' he whispered.

A light flashed and they breathed a sigh of relief. Nathalie estimated that Gilbert had taken twice as long as Pierre to pick the locks. Clearly he was not as skilled as he led them to believe.

'Come on,' Paul said, relieved to be on the move. 'Let's go.'

When they reached the steps, the door to the sewer was open but there were no escapees.

'*Merde!*' cursed Paul. 'Where are they?'

He took a few steps inside the entrance and listened. There was no sound of footsteps.

'We'll give them five minutes. If they're not here by then, we abort the mission.'

They listened for what seemed like an eternity, but the only noises they heard were the strange groaning and clanking sounds emanating towards them through the dark, dank and humid subterranean passageways. Nathalie was reminded of the scene in Victor Hugo's *Les Misérables,* where Jean Valjean carried the body of Marius into the sewers after a battle. Now she prayed there would be no bodies of their own.

When the five minutes was up, Paul shook his head in despair. 'Something has gone terribly wrong. The "package" has gone astray. We have to let the others know immediately.' He turned to Gilbert. 'Lock this door and put the chains back in place straight away. Nathalie, keep a lookout.'

She scrambled back up the stairs and was relieved to see the street still silent and empty.

'This is where we part ways,' Paul said to her. 'I want you to go back home immediately. Gilbert, you will come with me to warn the others.'

Nathalie took the circuitous route back to rue Frédéric Chopin and decided to wait in the shop until the Reynauds arrived back safe and sound. It was almost two in the morning and she was at her wit's end. The minutes ticked by. *What if they were all caught?* The Gestapo would come for her, and as much as she tried to be brave, she didn't think she would be able to withstand torture. The thought made her sick to the stomach. This was exactly what her parents had warned her against. This was the price of freedom.

She heard the door open. The Reynauds were back.

Antoine placed his gun on the table and pulled out a bottle of cognac. 'We all got away safely, thank God. Paul's gone to the safe house to see what's happened. He'll let us know in the morning. That is unless the Gestapo have got wind of us.'

He drank the cognac in one go and poured another. 'I'd better hide this,' he said picking up the gun, 'in case we have unexpected visitors.'

Mme Reynaud took it from him and looked around for somewhere to hide it. She picked up the nearest bucket, removed the container of flowers, and then slipped the gun inside placing the flowers back on top.

'We have Nathalie to thank for that clever idea,' she said.

For a brief moment, her comment raised a smile, but it would not last. With each hour that passed, their fears grew. At around seven o'clock in the morning, the telephone rang. Antoine answered it.

'*Oui.*'

Mme Reynaud and Nathalie watched his face.

'*Merci,*' he said, and slowly lowered the receiver.

The look on his face told them the news was bad. Mme Reynaud clasped her hands to her face.

'No, no, not again. We've been so careful.'

Nathalie bit her lip to stop herself from crying.

Several hours later, Paul arrived and told them what took place. The Gestapo had the safe house staked out. They waited until Sylvie entered and then raided it. The seven escapees all had forged identity cards, but under threat of execution, one of them admitted to being a Jew. They were immediately taken away to a holding area at Drancy. Paul's informants at the camp told him a train would be leaving for Poland that night and it was likely they would be on it.

'What about Sylvie?' asked Mme Reynaud.

Paul knitted his brows together and gave a painful sigh. 'She's been taken to Avenue Foch where she's probably being interrogated as we speak. We can only pray she won't break.'

'Then they still don't know about Pont de l'Alma and the barges?' she asked.

'Not yet. We can be thankful they hadn't reached the sewers. I'm sure that if they knew we were using the coal-barges, they would have waited to catch the men red-handed.'

The depth of despondency was written on his face. 'As for Sylvie,' he added, 'it's still an offence to aid Jews, let alone provide them with false documents. This is not something she can get out of easily. I wish to God I'd sent a man to the house instead of her. The escape was so meticulously planned, yet I can't help feeling responsible for them all. '

'You are not to blame,' Antoine said. 'We all agreed that a woman would appear less suspicious going to the house whilst the men waited nearby.'

'But they were not nearby, were they?' Paul replied. 'They were several streets away. She shouldn't have been alone.'

He looked at his watch. 'I must leave; I have other business to attend to. For the moment, all operations are cancelled until we see how this pans out.'

'What about the new IDs? Gilbert was supposed to collect them this week.'

Gilbert, Nathalie thought to herself. She recalled the raid after he'd dropped the other IDs off. And he was the only one to escape the night Anna was killed. She had a bad feeling about him but if she voiced this to the others, they would think her paranoid. Without proof, she could do nothing.

'Leave it to me,' he replied. 'I will pick them up myself.'

He turned his attention to Nathalie. 'Antoine told me you wanted to learn how to use a gun. In light of recent events, I think it's an excellent idea. In fact, we should all carry them from now on. Come to my house tomorrow and I will see what I can do for you.'

Over the next few days, Paul taught Nathalie everything he could about firearms. After several days of target practice in a disused warehouse, he gave her a small Pistolet wx, a Polish single-action, semi-automatic, known to be extremely reliable and accurate.

'You're an excellent shot, Mademoiselle Fontaine,' he said with a smile, 'but let's hope you never have to use it.'

CHAPTER EIGHT

The damp dark days of winter were well and truly over. Paris shed her winter mantel and her heart throbbed once again. The trees were in bloom, the nights warm, and café owners everywhere threw open their doors, lining the pavements with their little round tables and wicker-backed chairs.

Nathalie handed the waiter her last few francs and at the same time wondered how on earth she would get by. Throughout the winter, she had been frugal. Most of her money was spent on wood and the occasional sack of pine cones that the Reynauds had managed to get at the flower market. Now it was all gone. She couldn't ask her parents for more and neither could she borrow from the Reynauds who were feeling the pinch themselves. She had to find a job, but that was easier said than done. Businesses everywhere were suffering. Even the Reynauds could no longer afford to keep her on. The best flowers came at a premium which few could afford.

Passing a few hours in a sidewalk café had been one of her joys and after today, it seemed that would have to stop until she found a job. A young couple sat at a nearby table, holding hands and looking lovingly into each other's eyes. Nathalie felt a pang of jealousy. How she longed to be in their shoes, inhabiting a bubble in which only they mattered. Her thoughts drifted to Pierre. Madame Reynaud said he was back in Montmartre and she wished he would call to say hello.

Since Sylvie's execution, five days after she was interrogated at Avenue Foch, Paul decided the group was not to meet for a while. That was three weeks ago, but it had not stopped the odd person arriving at the shop seeking help. In every case, Paul had taken care of them, arranging their new IDs himself. His actions made Nathalie wonder if he suspected someone in the group to be a collaborator. If he did, he was keeping it very close to his chest.

A man's voice brought her back down to earth.

'Is this seat taken?' he asked, gesturing to the vacant chair next to her.

'That's fine,' Nathalie replied, 'I was about to leave anyway.'

'It's good to see people enjoying themselves again, isn't it?' the man continued.

She nodded in agreement. He appeared to want to chat and although he seemed friendly enough, she wasn't really in the mood for polite conversation. The man ordered a glass of champagne. He turned to Nathalie and asked if she would care to join him. The afternoon was too beautiful for her to waste and she accepted.

'In that case,' he said, addressing the waiter, 'make it a bottle. Veuve Clicquot.'

Nathalie looked surprised. Who on earth ordered a bottle of champagne in the middle of the afternoon – especially when times were tough? The waiter returned, poured them each a glass, and set the bottle in an ice bucket.

'To your health,' the man said, raising his glass.

After months of cheap red wine, the champagne was like honey and she savoured each sip with sheer delight.

'Do you live locally?' he asked.

She was about to point to the apartment above *La Vie en Fleurs*, which was in the same street, and then thought better of it.

'Not too far. And you?'

'I also live nearby.'

She studied him carefully. If he had been a lot younger, she might have thought he was trying to pick her up. He was middle-aged, possibly late fifties, an elegant man with fine dark hair greying at the temples, and a smooth olive complexion: the sort of man who took his holidays in the South of France or Biarritz. Judging by his clothes and his pleasant, self-confident air, she surmised him to be a man who belonged to the professional classes, maybe even an aristocrat. There were certainly plenty of those in the area. She had delivered flowers to them.

'Allow me to introduce myself,' he said, offering her his hand. 'My name is Chambrun – Lucien Chambrun.'

'Nathalie Fontaine.'

'Your accent, it's not Parisian.'

'No, I'm from the South.'

'And what brings you to Paris?'

'I came to visit my uncle. He's not been too well. I also thought it would give me chance to look for work.'

Chambrun refilled Nathalie's glass and then lit up a cigar. Judging by the bouquet it was a quality Cuban cigar, as befitted a man who would drink champagne in a café during the afternoon.

The aroma reminded her of her father. He always smoked one on special occasions.

'And were you successful?'

She blushed. 'I'm afraid not. The situation here is worse than I imagined.' She tried to sound naive. 'Maybe now that the warmer weather has arrived I will get a job as a waitress.'

'A waitress! My dear, I would have thought you could do much better than that.'

Beggars can't be choosers, she thought to herself, especially when you've just spent your last few francs on a coffee.

He studied Nathalie as she had studied him.

'I think I may be able to help you,' he said with a smile. 'A friend of mine is looking for someone to work a few hours a week.'

Nathalie looked surprised. She knew nothing about him and yet here he was, offering to help her. Who was he? More importantly, what was the job?

'Who is this friend?' she asked.

'I think you might have heard of him – Monsieur Jacques De Rossier.'

Nathalie was unable to hide her surprise. 'You mean De Rossier the Couturier?'

'The very same.'

'Are you trying to humour me, Monsieur?' she laughed.

'Indeed not. I happen to know he's looking for another model, and from the delightful picture I see in front of me, I think you would fit the bill admirably.'

Nathalie's hand fluttered across her knee as she smoothed down the folds of her blue and white cotton dress – the only good summer dress she possessed. People had often told her she was attractive, but model material, well that was something else.

'You have all the right qualities,' Chambrun continued. 'You not only have an excellent figure, but you are tall and charmingly beautiful, and you have a freshness that Jacques adores.'

Jacques! Nathalie smiled to herself. The way he referred to one of France's finest couturiers as if he was a good friend, amused her. Then she remembered that most of the couturiers had either closed their businesses, or left France when the Germans marched into Paris – except for Lucien Lelong and Chanel, who apparently was too busy with her German lover to bother designing clothes these days.

'How do you know this?' Nathalie asked.

'Jacques and I are old friends. He is most particular about the women he chooses to model for his clients. They must possess a certain elegance that complements their taste.' He reached for the champagne bottle and topped up her glass. 'You would think

49

finding a model would be easy, but most of those who apply are from the Pigalle – if you know what I mean?'

Nathalie knew exactly what he meant.

'I'm not sure...'

'Why don't you give him a call? It won't hurt. Tell him Lucien sent you.'

Chambrun took a piece of paper from his wallet and wrote De Rossier's name and telephone on it.

He got up to leave. 'And now, if you will excuse me, I must be getting along. Perhaps the next time we meet, your fortunes will have changed.'

They shook hands and he departed, leaving Nathalie thinking it was all a dream. Perhaps she would give De Rossier a call after all.

The Reynauds listened to Nathalie's story with a mixture of amusement and concern. The first thing that crossed their mind was that he might be a *mouchard* – a police informer.

'Where did you say you met him?' Mme Reynaud asked again.

'Café Voltaire. I was about to leave when he sat next to me and struck up a conversation.'

Mme Reynaud seemed suspicious. 'Nobody strikes up a conversation without a good reason,' she replied, rather frostily. 'People don't trust each other these days, especially if they are well-fed, well-dressed, and seemingly well-to-do, as you imply.'

Nathalie was relieved she hadn't told them they'd drunk champagne.

'I know the owner,' she continued. 'I will make some inquiries as to who he is. It's strange that he never told you where he lived.'

'I never told him where I lived either,' Nathalie replied. 'Perhaps he didn't say anything for the same reason you've just said: no-one trusts anyone anymore.'

Madame Reynaud knitted her eyebrows together. 'Alright,' she said. 'You can call De Rossier from here.'

Nathalie gave her a kiss on the cheek and dialled the number.

'*Bonjour,*' a woman's voice answered. 'How may I assist you?'

'I'd like to speak with Monsieur De Rossier, please.'

'And whom may I say is calling?'

'He doesn't know me. My name is Nathalie Fontaine. I'm an acquaintance of Monsieur Lucien Chambrun.'

The woman asked her to hold the line. The Reynauds listened anxiously.

After a few minutes a man's voice answered.

'This is Jacques. What can I do for you?'

At the sound of his voice, Nathalie was so excited she almost dropped the phone. She told him she was a friend of Lucien's and that he had told her De Rossier was looking for models. She would like to apply. There was a brief silence and he told her to call at his atelier the next day.

'10:00 am sharp.' De Rossier said. 'And don't be late. I abhor tardiness.'

The phone went dead.

Nathalie put her hands to her face in disbelief. 'I don't believe it,' she said with a huge grin. 'He wants to see me tomorrow morning.'

CHAPTER NINE

Nathalie arrived at La Maison de Jacques De Rossier in the rue du Faubourg Saint-Honoré at exactly five minutes to ten. A black Mercedes Benz was parked outside with a uniformed chauffeur standing nearby. When she got closer, she noticed the small, but unmistakable red Nazi flag with the black swastika, on the front of the bonnet. Madame Reynaud's warning about De Rossier being a collaborator rang loudly in her ear. It wasn't too late to turn back, but the feeling of utter desperation at having no money combined with a sense of curiosity, made her continue. When she reached the atelier, she took one look at the double-fronted doors, flanked by two marble torsos of female nudes, garlanded in a cornucopia of fruits, and felt a tingle of excitement run down her spine. Above the door was a coat of arms, the swirls of which were ornamented in gold. She had often admired such grand entrances on her walks through Paris, but never imagined she would ever have the occasion to step inside one of them.

A woman in a fox fur and carrying a Pekinese dog was just leaving. She walked towards the black car and sat in the back seat, elegantly sliding her long slim legs after her. Nathalie had a sinking feeling that she didn't belong here.

The entrance opened into an expansive hallway decorated in antiques and fine Persian carpets. Paintings and tapestries hung on the walls, and above her, hanging from a stuccoed ceiling, were three chandeliers that glittered like diamonds on an enormous spider web. A woman seated at a huge mahogany desk, was talking on the telephone and writing something down in a leather-bound appointment book. When she finished, she turned her attention to Nathalie.

'How may I help you?'

Nathalie recognized the voice. It was the same woman she had spoken with the day before.

'I have an appointment with Monsieur De Rossier.'

The woman double-checked the appointment book and asked her to follow her to a room on the first floor. She knocked and entered.

'Mademoiselle Nathalie Fontaine is here to see you, Monsieur.'

'Show her in.'

Jacques De Rossier was a small man in his forties with delicate features. Nathalie had seen photographs of him in fashion magazines. He always seemed shy, as if he purposely avoided the cameras, yet standing in front of him as she did now, she realized that wasn't so. He had a powerful presence which intimidated her. He got up from behind his desk and walked towards her.

'Let me look at you,' he said, in a forthright manner without even a word of introduction or welcome. 'Turn around.'

Nathalie twirled around on the carpet until he told her to stop.

'You've never modelled before, I take it?' he said, eyeing every inch of her.

'No, Monsieur.'

De Rossier walked over to a rack filled with dresses and pulled one out – a silver crepe-de-chine evening dress with a deep drape at the back.

'Put this on. Let me see what you look like.'

Nathalie looked around for somewhere to change.

'I can see you are the shy type,' he said with a smile. 'Go behind the rack, if you must, and take these.' He gave her a pair of embroidered satin shoes to match.

Her hands were clammy with nerves as she took off her own simple, cotton dress and slipped effortlessly into the elegant one. The dress was so low at the back that she could not wear a bra which caused her great embarrassment, although the feel of the fabric against her partially naked body was heaven. It didn't need a bra. There was no mirror and she had no idea what she looked like, but she did know she felt transformed; more confident. When she walked back out, De Rossier was sitting on the edge of his desk waiting for her. A smile crossed his lips.

'Walk up and down,' he ordered. 'And keep your head high.'

She did this several times whilst he watched her carefully, occasionally making a comment about where to look and how to hold her shoulders.

'Now, do it again, and this time don't make eye contact. Models are not allowed to make eye contact with the clients during a showing. They must remain aloof at all times.'

When he was satisfied with her walk, he circled her and brushed his hand through her hair holding it away from her face in order to see her neck and full profile.

'You may not be aware, young lady, but you have quite an aristocratic face, and with a few lessons, you could also have an aristocratic bearing. That would please my customers very much.'

He picked up a bolt of midnight blue silk from a chair, pulled away a few metres and draped it over her shoulder.

'Magnificent. You will be the one to wear this exquisite piece.'

He picked up the telephone and asked his premier vendeuse to come in. Almost immediately, a well dressed young woman with blond hair came into the room. He handed her the bolt of fabric.

'This is Mademoiselle Nathalie Fontaine. She is to be our new model. I want you to take her measurements. She will wear this for the Countess Irené next week.' He shook Nathalie's hand and returned to his desk. 'Mme Lefort will look after you. I will see you next Wednesday.' He returned to his desk. 'And another thing, Margaux, find something for Mademoiselle Fontaine to wear in the meantime. The frock she is wearing is most unflattering.'

Mme Lefort picked up Nathalie's clothes and ushered her out of the room.

Once outside, Nathalie let out a sigh of relief.

'Yes, he can be rather intimidating,' Mme Lefort smiled, 'but you don't have to worry, he is a pussy cat when he likes someone, and he obviously likes you.'

'Do you think so? I've never done any modelling before. I don't know if I will be any good. I've never even thought of myself as having the right looks either.'

'You don't have to worry. You'll soon get the hang of it. Besides, it's not as if we have collections to put out every year now.'

Mme Lefort took Nathalie into the sewing room where there were half a dozen seamstress busily working on large sewing tables and pinning fabrics on papier-mâché mannequins.

'Why are there no more big collections now?' Nathalie asked innocently. 'I would have thought the magazines would have loved that sort of thing. It's a diversion from the occupation.'

'The magazines, yes: not the public. Most of them think we should have shut up shop.'

'Then what will I be doing?'

'Monsieur De Rossier has many personal clients who keep us busy. These clients require personal showings. Maybe two or three models are used, rarely more.'

After Nathalie's measurements had been recorded, Mme Lefort looked through several racks in the room, and pulled out a few clothes: two dresses, two skirts and blouses and last of all, two sets of pale blue, lace-edged silk underwear.

'The Monsieur believes that for a woman to feel like a *real* woman – sensuous and feminine – she must wear the correct lingerie,' she said, wrapping them in black tissue paper. 'He always tells us that his creations are designed only for goddesses, and in his opinion, a woman will feel like a goddess if she wears these.'

Nathalie was speechless. The clothes cost a small fortune. They returned to the reception where Mme Lefort told the receptionist to book her in for two appointments the following week.

'I want you to come back on Wednesday, that's the day before the showing. I will run you through everything. The showing will be the next day.'

'There's just one small thing,' Nathalie said when they were out of earshot of the receptionist. 'I have no idea of the salary. Monsieur De Rossier never mentioned it.'

'He doesn't like to talk about money,' Mme Lefort replied, haughtily. 'It's the way he is. He leaves the money matters to others. However, I can assure you that you will be well-paid. I will personally take care of it.' Nathalie thanked her. 'And of course,' Mme Lefort added. 'There's the little matter of your new outfits. I'm sure you will agree that they alone are worth a small sum.'

They shook hands and Nathalie stepped back out into the rue du Faubourg Saint-Honoré as if in a dream. She couldn't believe what was happening to her.

The Reynauds were eager to hear what had taken place. When she placed the bag on the table and pulled out the designer clothes, Mme Reynaud clapped her hands together in shock.

'*Mon Dieu!*' She picked up the lingerie and fingered it gently. 'I have never seen anything so beautiful.'

'And did they tell you what sort of salary you would be getting?' Monsieur Reynaud asked.

'Not exactly. Except that I will be well-paid.'

Monsieur Reynaud frowned. 'Let us hope you will be well and truly recompensed. Working for a collaborator will have its drawbacks.'

'What drawbacks might those be?' Nathalie asked, coming back to earth with a thud.

'When this war ends, people will remember who worked for the Germans, mark my word.'

CHAPTER TEN

The following day, Paul called at the Reynauds for dinner. He had a new assignment for Nathalie.

'There's a man I want you to accompany as far as Tours. I think you will suit the job perfectly,' he said, lighting up a Gitane. 'He's someone very important and it's vital we get him out of Paris as soon as possible.'

The first thing Nathalie thought of was her new job. If she failed to turn up on Wednesday, that would be the end of it. And then there was the matter of the clothes. She would look like a thief.

Paul read her mind. 'Madeleine told me about your new job and I think we can work our way around it. If you leave on Saturday, you should be back by Tuesday at the latest. It should only take a couple of hours to get there, but I would like you to stay the night, possibly even two.'

'May I ask who this man is?'

'You will know him as René Hubert and he will be your husband.'

Nathalie's eyes widened. The Reynauds listened without uttering a word.

He took an envelope from his jacket pocket and pushed it

across the table towards her. She picked it up and emptied out the contents. In it were two false identity cards, a marriage certificate dated a month earlier, two tickets, and an *Ausweis* each – a travel pass. She looked at René's photograph. He was a handsome man, and according to the date on his ID, he was thirty-one years old. She looked at her own. She was to be Madame Camille Hubert, age twenty-four, from a village outside of Tours.

'Your ruse will be that you have just recently married, and René has volunteered to go to work in Germany on behalf of the French government. He has volunteered to work for the betterment of Vichy France and the Fatherland because the factory where he worked on the outskirts of Paris was bombed by Allied Aircraft, killing his comrades. You are both travelling to Tours because you want him to meet your parents before he goes away.' He studied her face. 'Any questions?'

She leafed through the IDs and several pages of notes.

'Study the information with the IDs and then destroy it. One more thing, the name, Camille, is also your code name. It will only be used when you come in contact with one of our agents. At some time during your stay in Tours, someone will direct you to a place where you will meet one of them. The message will be carefully worded, so please be on the lookout for it. Follow the instructions carefully and the agent will meet up with you. This person will not address you as Nathalie, only Camille. If he does not address you as such, he will not be one of our own. In which case, you must consider you could be compromised and act accordingly.'

Paul finished his cigarette and glanced towards Mme Reynaud. 'There's one other thing. This new job of yours, I applaud you for getting it, but I am in agreement with Madeleine. De Rossier is a collaborator. However, if we take great care, we can turn that to our advantage. Think of it as another little assignment,' he said.

'What do you have in mind?'

'Make a note of everyone you come in contact with – a mental note, you understand. Under no circumstances are you to write anything down. I want to know who his clients are, and anyone else – including the mysterious man from Café Voltaire who helped you to get the job.'

Nathalie looked at the Reynauds.

Mme Reynaud shrugged. 'I'm sorry, Nathalie. We have to be careful. We have a responsibility to your father to take care of you. I know the proprietor of Café Voltaire well and I checked with him. He'd never seen the man before so he couldn't possibly live around here.'

'The café was packed,' Nathalie replied, with a tinge of annoyance. 'Surely you can't expect him to remember everyone who goes there? He probably doesn't even remember me?'

'His café is in this street. We *all* know each other. He knew who you were from the moment you moved in. The street has eyes. *Every* street has eyes. It will pay you to remember that.'

Nathalie felt her cheeks redden. Mme Reynaud was an enigma. On the one hand she could be the motherly, gentle type, and on the other – like now – as tough as any man, chastising her for letting her guard down.

'That's it then,' Paul said. 'Now, no more talk about work. Let's enjoy our dinner.'

Mme Reynaud excelled herself that evening. She had managed to acquire a fat hen in exchange for several bunches of roses, and roasted it to perfection. Yet, try as she might, Nathalie could not take her mind off the events of the day. The thought of doing a little modelling for a famous couturier was appealing, but she didn't want to be labelled a collaborator.

When she retired to her room, she looked at the documents Paul had given her, going over them in her mind until she was satisfied she'd committed them to memory. Then she struck a match and let the notes burn in the empty wood burner.

On Saturday morning, Nathalie walked into a bar across the road from Gare Montparnasse with her suitcase, and looked for the man who was now her husband. René was sitting at a far table drinking a coffee. When he saw her, he came over.

'Ah, there you are,' he said, planting a kiss on her lips. 'I was worried about you.'

He called the waiter over, ordered two Vermouths, and asked if she would like a bite to eat before the departure. Nathalie was too nervous to think about eating. René reached across the table and took both her hands and brought them to his lips, kissing them tenderly.

'You look beautiful, my darling.'

She was wearing one of the new outfits Mme Lefort had given her, a figure-hugging apricot rayon dress, with a cross-over bodice that emphasized her bust and small waist. Around her neck, she wore her pearls. They made her think of Pierre. She wondered if he had any idea of what she was doing and if he would approve. Underneath the dress, she wore the luxurious pale blue lace and silk underwear. De Rossier was right when he said good lingerie transformed a woman. She did indeed feel like a goddess.

René continued to talk to her in an endearing way, but he could see she was slightly uncomfortable. He leaned over and whispered in her ear.

'Those men on that table are Gestapo. They've been here a while now and I believe they are looking for someone. So please, my darling, do pretend to love me.'

Before she could answer, he kissed her again and this time she responded more warmly. In just five minutes of being in his company, he had managed to put her at ease. She even managed a smile, which pleased him enormously.

René was an attractive man with chestnut hair and dark eyes which shone when he smiled. Paul had said he was someone important to their network and she was intrigued. Hopefully there would be time enough to get to know him a little more over the weekend, although she knew they were both bound to a code of silence.

They finished the aperitif and left for the station. Knowing the difficulty they would have to face before they got on the train, Nathalie's heart started to beat fiercely, and she found herself looping her arm through his and rubbing her body close to him. Acting as naturally as possible, they stopped to buy a newspaper from a kiosk, right under the noses of the French police. She looked at his face and he gave her a reassuring smile. They were checked three times before finally boarding the train. Paul's forger had done an excellent job.

They were travelling on first-class tickets, which meant that they would not have to spend the trip in cramped conditions. On the other hand, German officers travelled first class. It was a risk Paul had been prepared to take. René placed their suitcases on the luggage rack and they took their seat next to the window. Nathalie would not be able to relax until they had left the station. Until then, anything could go wrong. She looked at the bustling crowd on the platform and surveyed their faces, a habit she had become accustomed to. Random searches were still taking place, and she half expected the Gestapo to open the door and haul them outside at any moment.

'Look,' René said, 'over there. It's the same men who were in the café.'

Nathalie took a quick look. 'You're right, and they're coming this way.' She slumped back into her seat. 'I can't look. What if they were on to us all the time?'

René drew his face away from the window and opened up his newspaper, glancing outside each time he turned a page. The men walked past each compartment, casting an eye up at the windows and occasionally stopping to talk to a guard. Eventually, they disappeared and the pair breathed a sigh of relief.

'I feel as though I have "guilty" stamped across my forehead,' Nathalie said.

René laughed. 'I can see you're a novice at this sort of thing, but you're doing fine.'

Nathalie wondered if the escapes she'd taken part in, along with the many drop-offs she'd made as a courier for Mme Reynaud, still made her a novice. Not to mention that she was now able to use a firearm. When the train departed, they were relieved to find they were alone and they passed the time in small talk like old friends. She was beginning to like her *husband*.

The hotel in Tours was within walking distance from the railway station. It had been booked for two nights. The concierge looked at their documents and showed them to their room. It was small and cramped with only one bed, but it did have a bath which they were thankful for.

'We serve breakfast from seven onwards,' the man told them. 'As we have no restaurant, my wife will bring it to your room.'

When he'd gone, Nathalie sank down on the bed. It was as hard as nails.

'What are we going to do about the sleeping arrangements?' she asked, looking rather embarrassed. 'Shall we take it in turns to use the bed; you one night, me the other?'

She looked in the cupboard and saw there was an extra blanket and pillow.

'I will take the chair,' René said. 'You are welcome to the bed.'

Nathalie had little to hang up. She had brought the second dress Madame Lefort gave her and that was all. René decided to have a bath and Nathalie settled down on the bed to read a book. It was going to be a long two days. At the end of that time, someone was to meet them and René would be gone – a mere flash in her life. He left the bathroom door partially open and she could hear the splashing of water. She couldn't concentrate and put the book down. He seemed so carefree.

After a while, he returned to the room wrapped in a towel. She was about to tell him he could stop the play acting now and get dressed until he put his finger on his lips and moved closer to the door, turning the key in the lock and listening carefully.

'How about we go and find a nice restaurant, my darling?' he asked, in a raised voice. 'We must make the most of our few days together. Soon I will be in Germany and who knows when we will see each other again. There's a restaurant across the road. Let's ask the concierge if it's any good.'

'I would like that,' Nathalie replied.

When he was sure all was fine, he stepped away from the door.

'What was all that about?' Nathalie asked. 'You scared me.'

He sat on the side of the bed. He smelt of cheap soap and eau-de-cologne.

'I thought I heard footsteps in the corridor. The Gestapo will want to know who is staying here, and it's likely the manager will be giving them our details right now. We must act like a married couple or we will attract suspicion.' He lifted her chin towards him with his finger. 'And besides, I like you... too much, I'm afraid.'

Nathalie moved her head to the side to avoid looking into his eyes, but he pulled her face back and kissed her hard on the lips. Whether it was the warm sun streaming through the window, the smell of fresh eau-de-cologne, the lace and silk lingerie she was wearing, or simply a frisson of excitement at being a part of something so dangerous, she wasn't sure. All she knew was, she was attracted to this stranger and his touch excited her. This is what she had longed for with Pierre. Over the past few months, those pent-up emotions had consumed her. And now, here she was with a stranger, reciprocating his affections without a second thought, allowing them to spill over in a deluge of lust.

As their passion increased, he stood up and pulled off her dress, revealing the luxurious lingerie on her slender body. The look and feel of it excited him all the more, until in the end, he removed that also. When she was completely naked, he pulled her on top of him. Nathalie had never experienced such passion as this before. Wild and soft at the same time, she gave herself to him as if she had known him for ages. When it was over, they lay wrapped in each other's arms. There were no apologies, no regrets, just a warm sensation of belonging to someone else for however precious time they had together.

René propped himself up on the pillow and watched her dress.

'Well, Monsieur Hubert,' Nathalie said, with a cheeky smile, 'your *wife* is famished. What are you going to do about it?'

He pulled her back on to the bed and smothered her neck in kisses. 'I am going to eat her, that's what.'

Nathalie slapped him playfully. 'Do you treat all your *wives* in this manner?' she laughed.

'I've only been married once and I'm beginning to like it.'

It was in this happy and playful mood that the pair went out to dine, keeping up the pretence of being happy newlyweds. The weather was beautiful and the setting romantic. Soft lights and small vases of wildflowers decorated the tables, which had been laid with crisp white tablecloths. The menu was sparse and what it lacked in food, it provided in atmosphere. Nathalie ordered the omelette and a salad, and René ordered chicken. The waiter recommended a good local wine which they were only too happy to try. Seeing that the couple were very much in love, he told them it was on the house. It took them all their time not to burst out laughing.

'I know nothing about you?' René said, kissing her hand. 'Not even your real name? I wish I did.'

'Then we are even,' Nathalie replied. 'All I know about you is that you are an important man.'

He laughed. 'Let's say I have an important role to play at the moment. We'll leave it at that and enjoy our moment together.'

In the morning, they were woken by a soft knock on the door. The concierge's wife had brought them breakfast. René threw on some clothes and told her to leave the tray on the table by the window.

'It's going to be a beautiful day again, I believe,' she said, glancing towards Nathalie, who had pulled the sheets around her in an attempt at maintaining a little modesty. 'Do you have any plans to go sightseeing, Mme Camille? Maybe the church would be a good place to start. It's not too far away.'

Nathalie let her words sink in. Was this the coded message Paul had told her she would receive? The woman had referred to her as Mme Camille, *and* she had told her where to go.

'Thank you. That sounds like a good idea,' she replied.

The woman smiled at her and left the room. Nathalie sat down to eat her breakfast – a solitary boiled egg and fresh bread. There was no butter, and conserves were scarce. Knowing that the woman would have been standing in a long queue well before dawn, they considered themselves lucky to even to have fresh bread.

'I might go for a walk to the church this morning,' Nathalie said. 'Maybe we can do something together this afternoon.'

René looked at her thoughtfully. He was well aware that if she wanted to go alone, then she had a good reason for it.

Nathalie arrived at the church just as the parishioners were leaving after mass. She took a stroll through the adjoining graveyard until everyone had left and then stepped inside the church. The priest was standing by the altar. When he heard her footsteps, he came over.

'How can I help you?'

'I've come to confess, Father.'

The priest closed the church door and ushered her into the confession box. When he addressed her as Camille, she let out a sigh of relief.

'The man you have with you,' the priest continued. 'He is to leave Tours in the early hours of the morning.' He gave her an address of a safe house not far from their hotel. 'Can you make sure he gets there before curfew?'

'I'll do my very best.'

'There's no room for mistakes, Camille. There will be a small plant pot on the windowsill to denote all is well. If it is not there, walk on.'

'How will I know he has left Tours safely?'

They paused for a moment and heard the church doors open.

'Come to the church before you depart for Paris,' the priest replied.

The conversation barely lasted three minutes. When they emerged from the confession box, two well-dressed men in suits had entered the church and were standing in the doorway. Nathalie's heart missed a beat, but the priest assured her everything was fine.

'They like to pay me a visit every now and then,' he smiled. 'I'm used to them.'

The priest made the sign of the cross over her forehead and said goodbye. Nathalie walked past them, smiling sweetly. They, in turn, lifted their hats and bid her a good day. It never ceased to amaze her how polite and gracious the Gestapo could be when they wanted to.

René was lying on the bed when Nathalie returned. 'How was your sight-seeing?' he asked.

'Fruitful.' she replied, looking out of the window and trying to hide the emotion in her voice.

He came over and turned her to face him. 'I gather by your face, our time has come to an end.'

She laid her head on his shoulder. 'We knew what we were getting into.'

'Then let us enjoy our last moments together.'

They spent one more meal together and a few hours before curfew, returned to the hotel and made love one last time.

'Time to go,' Nathalie said after a while. 'Or we'll be late.'

She slipped her dress back on, went over to her suitcase and took out an envelope. 'One more thing; I have been asked to give you this,' she said. 'To tide you over until you get to your final destination.'

In the envelope was ten thousand francs.

It was well and truly dark by the time they arrived at the safe house. The plant pot was still on the windowsill. René drew her into his arms and gave her one last kiss.

'I'm proud to have known you, Camille,' he said, tenderly.

'And I you.'

'You won't forget me, will you?'

'Never,' Nathalie replied, trying to hide the emotion in her voice. 'Now go before somebody sees us. And take care.'

He picked up his suitcase and knocked on the door whilst Nathalie waited in the shadows to check all was well. Then he was gone. He had disappeared from her life as quickly as he had entered it; a *petite affaire* by two lonely people who yearned for affection and grabbed it while they could. *Fate is cruel*, she thought to herself, as she made her way back to the hotel.

The following morning, she passed by the church on her way to the station.

The priest gave her a broad smile. 'All went well, Camille. Our friend will be well and truly on his way by now.'

CHAPTER ELEVEN

Mme Lefort gave the finished dress to Nathalie to try on. After a slight adjustment to the waistline, it fitted perfectly.

'Now I want you to walk up and down the room,' she said, taking a seat. 'Imagine that I am the customer and you want to please me.'

Nathalie took a deep breath, lifted her shoulders back, and proceeded to walk towards her. At first she felt stiff and wooden, until the vendeuse quickly put her at ease by telling her to imagine she was going to meet her lover by the Seine. Thoughts of René and Tours flashed through her mind, but after a while René's face faded and was replaced by Pierre's. She imagined she was going to meet him and the look on his face told her he had missed her.

'Well done,' Mme Lefort said. 'Much better, but do try and remember what the Monsieur told you. Don't look at the client.'

After a few hours of catwalk lessons combined with deportment, she went over the events that would take place the next day.

'You are to be here at three o'clock. The clients will arrive an hour later and will have drinks and chat with Monsieur De

Rossier first. After that the showing will begin. There will be two other models with you – Chantelle and Monique. They have been with the House of De Rossier since before the war and know the ropes well. There will also be someone to help you with your hair and make-up.'

Mme Lefort turned Nathalie's head towards the light. 'You have a good bone structure and flawless skin which our clientele like. And if I might say, there is a warm glow about your face – and a sparkle in your eyes. That sparkle wasn't there when we met last time.'

Nathalie smiled. Mme Lefort was certainly observant.

'Do you mind if I ask who your clients will be? I feel rather nervous at being in the same room as...' she stopped mid-sentence.

'You mean Germans? We cannot always help who we do business with. Surely you must know that?'

Nathalie blushed.

'The House of De Rossier is well-known. The Monsieur will design for anyone who appreciates his work – and if that means the wives and mistresses of Nazis, then so be it. They pay well. Besides, there are still French ladies of means who need to keep up appearances – even if we are at war. Monsieur De Rossier has a motto. *"We will not be sullied by war. That is to be left on the doorstep. Once our clients step inside, life will be as it always was; elegant and refined."'*

She handed Nathalie an envelope with several hundred francs in it, together with a pair of silk stockings and a bottle of Perfume. Nathalie couldn't hide her shock.

'Are you sure there hasn't been a mistake,' she asked. 'I mean, I haven't actually done anything yet. Then there's the matter of the clothes you gave me – and now this.'

Mme Lefort laughed. *'Ma chérie,* I told you that the Monsieur likes you. You have a certain style. Just one more little thing,' she added. 'One reason we look after our staff well is so that they will not divulge what goes on here to anyone.'

'I'm not sure that I understand.'

Mme Lefort's charm was suddenly replaced by a coldness that caught Nathalie off-guard.

'Under no circumstances are you to discuss our clientele with anyone. Is that understood?'

'Of course, you have my word,' Nathalie replied, knowing full well she had no intention of keeping that promise.

In a flash, Mme Lefort's cold look was replaced by a broad smile again. *Bien*. Then we will see you tomorrow afternoon.'

Later that evening, Paul passed by *La Vie en Fleurs* to talk to her about the assignment in Tours.

'Congratulations,' he said. 'You were excellent. René arrived safely in Lyons and sends you his regards.'

'What is so important about him?' she asked, half expecting him to dismiss her question.

'He's been sent by Général Charles De Gaulle himself as one of his top men. He and a few other select people are uniting the Résistance groups. We will be more effective under one banner.'

Nathalie smiled to herself. The news didn't exactly come as a surprise. René was a charming man and she felt sure he would be successful.

'I'm only too happy to have helped.'

'I gather that the Gestapo were in the bar where you met, and that you saw them again on the platform before the train pulled out?'

'The priest in Tours is also being watched. I was lucky they didn't bother me.'

Paul tapped his fingers on the table. 'We have to be vigilant, Nathalie. Too many odd things are happening; things that simply can't be put down to coincidences.'

She wanted to ask what he meant. Did he really suspect a traitor in their midst? What did he think about Gilbert? She refrained. He asked her how her day was at the House of De Rossier. She didn't tell him how much money she'd been given.

'The vendeuse is a tough woman. She can be most charming when she wants to, but today I saw the cold side of her. She made it clear I was not to divulge the names of his clients.'

'You'd better be careful then. She'll be watching you.'

The subject changed to a new cache of guns the Allies had parachuted into Normandy.

'If you have time, I'd like to have a few more sessions with my gun,' Nathalie said. 'I have quite a bit of time on my hands and I want to perfect my accuracy.'

'Good idea. Let me know when and we'll arrange something.'

It was still early when Paul left and Nathalie decided to pay Pierre a visit. Contacting another member of the group without good reason was not encouraged, so she decided it would be best not to tell the Reynauds. She wore her new clothes and dabbed a little perfume on her wrists and behind her ears. The fragrance was wonderful and she wished she'd worn it for René.

When she reached Pierre's apartment, Jean was clearing a table in the bistro and spotted her through the window. He stepped outside and told her he left a few hours earlier.

'Do you know where I can find him?'

'He took his easel and paints, so you could try the Place du Tertre. He often goes there to paint,' Jean replied.

On such a pleasant evening, the square was crowded with both Germans and Parisians. Bars and restaurants were bursting with patrons and artists, and musicians were doing their best to earn a few francs to get them through the next week. Jean was right; Pierre had set up his easel in the centre of the square along with other painters and souvenir sellers. Her heart raced when she saw him. As she walked through the crowd, she saw two men approach. Thinking they were buying a painting, she decided to wait until they moved on. The men didn't seem interested in his work. Instead they appeared to be having an animated conversation. After Pierre threw his hands in the air and returned to his painting, they left.

What was all that about, Nathalie asked herself? She walked over and took him by surprise.

'Good evening, Pierre.'

'Nathalie! You're the last person I expected to see.' He stood up and kissed her on the cheek. For a minute she thought he might say he'd missed her, but he appeared rather cool and she felt embarrassed, as if she'd intruded into his space.

'I see you didn't bring any flowers this time,' he said with a smile. 'Does that mean it's an unofficial visit?'

'You could say that. It's such a beautiful evening, I thought I'd come and say hello.' She looked at the painting he was working on. 'It's lovely,' she added.

It was a watercolour of one of the restaurants; a lively portrayal of people sitting at the outdoor tables having a good time.

'It reminds me of a Utrillo. It has the same liveliness.'

Pierre thanked her, adding that Utrillo was a great favourite with the painters in Montmartre.

'For a moment I thought you might have had an interested buyer – those two men who were here a minute ago.'

At the mention of the men, his smile faded. 'Oh those; they wanted it for nothing,' he snapped, and changed the subject. 'Have you eaten?'

'No, but I'm famished.'

'Where do you want to go?

'What about *Le Lapin Agile*?'

He laughed loudly. 'That's a favourite haunt of the Germans these days. Do you want to mix with them? It may spoil your appetite.'

'I will be the judge of that.'

'Fine. Give me a moment to pack these things away and drop them back at the apartment.'

He asked her to wait outside, which both surprised and

disappointed her. He was gone a full ten minutes during which time, she began to think she'd made a fool of herself by coming here. When he returned, she saw he was wearing the same clothes he wore on the occasion they went to the cinema. It raised her spirits as he had obviously made an effort for her.

Le Lapin Agile was packed and people were queuing outside although it was evident that anyone with a German uniform was able to get in.

'Wait here,' Pierre said. 'I know the manager.'

He disappeared and once again Nathalie was left standing outside with everyone else. A black limousine drove towards them and pulled up outside the entrance. The chauffeur got out and opened the door for a middle-aged man and a young woman.

'*Mon Dieu!*' she said to herself. 'It can't be!'

She found herself trying to blend in with the rest of the people in the queue in case she was spotted, but the man was too occupied with the young woman to notice her. She took a closer look as they walked through the door. It was definitely Lucien Chambrun, and the woman he was with didn't look much older than herself.

A few minutes later, Pierre reappeared. 'Are you alright? You look as though you've seen a ghost.'

'I'm fine. I thought I saw an old friend, but I was mistaken, that's all.'

'We're in luck,' he told her. 'The manager found us a table.'

'Perhaps we should go somewhere else?' Nathalie suggested. 'You might be right; maybe there will be too many Germans for my liking, after all.'

Pierre knitted his eyebrows together in a frown. 'Come on,' he said, taking her arm. 'You can't change your mind now. Besides, there are Germans everywhere in Montmartre at this time of night.'

They were shown to a table for two near the stage where three girls wearing skimpy outfits and headdresses of ostrich feathers were doing a bawdy song and dance act. Nathalie looked nervously around the darkened room for Chambrun. She breathed a sigh of relief when she couldn't see him.

'What will you have to drink?' Pierre asked.

'Champagne. Let's get a bottle.'

He sat back and whistled. 'Ooh la la! Such extravagance!'

'This is on me,' Nathalie replied. 'It's my treat.'

'Well, well, we are splashing out.'

She was amused at his response, and pleased that he had lightened up.

'You look stunning tonight, Nathalie,' he said, lighting up cigarettes for them both. 'The dress you are wearing is exquisite.' He leaned across the table, took her hand and kissed it. '*And* you also smell utterly delightful. What has happened to you since we last met? Where has that shy girl gone? And how can you afford to pay for such extravagance?'

'I have a new job and I would like to celebrate with someone.'

'I thought you already had a job at *La Vie en Fleurs*?'

'The Reynauds have been struggling to pay me for quite a while. In fact they only gave me a job to help me out. This is different. I found some modelling work. It's only a few days a week. Not even that really, but the pay is good and we all know that's hard to come by these days.'

'Perhaps you will model again for me one day?' he said, with a twinkle in his eye.

Nathalie slapped his hand playfully. 'No, this is modelling for one of the couturiers in the rue du Faubourg Saint-Honoré.'

Pierre's eyes widened. 'Which one?'

'The House of De Rossier!'

His smile disappeared. 'You should be careful of men like him?'

Nathalie was hurt by his reaction. She had expected a more enthusiastic response.

'You sound like Paul,' she replied, tersely.

'Do I? And what did he have to say when he found out?'

'That we can use it to our advantage.'

Pierre studied her for a few seconds. 'How does he propose you do that?'

'By noting all the people De Rossier deals with, especially his clientele.'

'How did you find this job? They're not exactly advertised.'

She leaned closer to him. 'That's the strange thing. I was having coffee at Café Voltaire just over a week ago, when this man sat next to me. We started talking and he asked me what I did for a living. I told him I was looking for a job, and he happened to mention that his friend was looking for a model. He thought I would fit the bill and gave me the number. De Rossier himself interviewed me and I was given the job.'

'Just like that?' Pierre answered.

'Well, what's wrong with that?' Nathalie was beginning to get fed up with his moodiness.

'Yes; just like that!' she snapped. 'Now, are you going to interrogate me, or are we going to enjoy ourselves?'

'Who was this man?'

Nathalie sighed. 'You are beginning to exasperate me, Pierre. I can't recall his name,' she lied.

She changed the subject and asked about his trip but he was reluctant to talk about it. This was another rule in the group; members didn't involve their families. Nathalie realized she's overstepped the mark and asked about his painting.

'Did you manage to sell a few more pieces?'

'Thankfully, yes. I also sold the painting I did of you.'

She looked disappointed as she'd hoped he was keeping it to remind him of her.

'Oh! I thought you said it wasn't for sale.'

'A buyer saw my paintings in the Place du Tertre. He bought one and wanted to see what else I had. I took him back to the apartment and when he saw it, he made an offer.'

'I see.'

'The man offered quite a substantial amount. I can always

paint another one of you – that is, if you are willing to sit for me again?'

Nathalie was just about to say yes when she became aware of someone coming towards their table.

'My dear Mademoiselle Fontaine, what a pleasure to see you again, and if I may say so, you are looking most delightful.'

Nathalie felt her heart pounding in her chest. 'Monsieur Chambrun!'

Before she could say anything else, he turned towards Pierre and extended his hand. 'And this lucky gentleman would be...'

Their eyes met. Pierre looked at him with a steely coldness, not uttering a word. The tension was palpable and his reaction scared her. For a minute she thought he was going to make a scene.

'Pierre,' she said, with a sweet smile, trying to defuse the situation. 'This is Monsieur Chambrun, the kind gentleman I was just telling you about.'

Still Pierre said nothing. Chambrun turned his attention back to Nathalie.

'I hear it worked out well for you. Allow me to congratulate you.'

'Thank you. I am indebted to you.'

Chambrun waved his hand in the air. 'Nonsense my dear.' His eyes fell on the champagne and he smiled. 'I will bid you both a good night. Enjoy yourselves.'

After he left, Nathalie leaned towards him. 'You were embarrassingly rude,' she whispered, her voice bursting with anger. 'What on earth is the matter with you? You have been involved with the group too long. It's making you paranoid.'

Pierre lit up another cigarette. 'You have no idea who that man is, do you?'

'Well, you're obviously about to tell me,' she replied sarcastically.

'His name is not Chambrun – its François Corneille and he belongs to the *Bureau des Menees Antinationals*, otherwise known as BMA, the "Bureau of Anti-National Activities". They were set up to oppose communist and resistance efforts. He reports to the Gestapo.' He sat back in his chair and sighed deeply.

Nathalie let his words sink in and then reached for her bag. 'I've lost my appetite. Let's get out of here.'

She called the waiter over and paid their bill. Chambrun – or Corneille, as she now knew he was called, was nowhere to be seen. Pierre could see she was distressed and offered to walk her to the metro.

'I didn't tell him where I lived,' Nathalie said, when they were outside. 'I was careful about that.'

'Did you give your details to De Rossier?'

Her face paled. 'I gave them to Madame Lefort, his vendeuse.' She stopped and grabbed his arm. 'Oh God, Pierre, what have I done?'

'It's good that you know all this. Now you can be extra vigilant. Just be careful what you say in your new job. Act naive.'

She laughed. 'I am naive aren't I? *Very* naive.'

They passed a small alleyway. He pulled her into it, pushed her against the wall and started to kiss her. After their heated conversations and his moodiness, his actions took her by surprise and she almost slapped his face, but the flame that she held for him was far too strong, and she found herself succumbing to his affections. They heard approaching footsteps and he quickly drew away from her and ran his hand through his hair whilst she smoothed down her dress. The footsteps turned out to be an old woman carrying a loaf of bread.

'*Bon soir,*' the woman said, as she passed.

'Bon soir,' Nathalie replied, suppressing a smile.

Pierre looked at his watch. 'It's only an hour until curfew. You'd better get a move on if you're going to catch that train."

'You're right,' she replied, disappointed that he didn't ask her to stay the night.

Instead he put his arm around her and whispered in her ear.

'Perhaps its best if we keep tonight's conversation between the two of us.'

She looked at him. 'You mean not tell the Reynauds or Paul?'

'I mean tell no-one. After all, it would only worry them, and they've got enough to deal with as it is.'

Nathalie was unsure. 'Paul specifically asked me to give him the names of De Rossier's clients and associates.'

'Then do as he asks, but I'd like you to tell me also. It will make me feel better.' He kissed her hard on the lips. 'Will you promise me that, Nathalie?'

She kissed him back. 'I promise,' she replied.

CHAPTER TWELVE

De Rossier's Salon was the epitome of bourgeois elegance; an eclectic mix of 19th century decorative styles, most of which were either Baroque Revival of France's Second Empire, or Neo-classiscm. A row of eight floor to ceiling windows, all of which opened out on to a small balcony overlooking the rue du Faubourg Saint-Honoré, were decorated in patterned, pale-blue silk damask drapes, secured with rope-and-tassel tie-backs, that matched an array of armchairs, sofas, and chaise lounges. To give added depth, the walls were covered with magnificent, gilt-framed mirrors which, together with the chandeliers, illuminated the room in a radiant glow. In less than an hour, this sumptuous salon would host a small, but elite party of Paris's most important socialites, all eager to catch a glimpse of the Master's creations. Nathalie was taken aback at such splendour. Growing up in a small village, she was not used to such elegance. Whilst millions suffered, the lives of those she would be modelling for would hardly have changed.

The catering staff set up a table of food and champagne, and Mme Lefort walked the girls through the timetable of events.

'You will walk through that door and along this carpet,' she said, waving her arm through the air. 'The guests will be seated here.' She indicated to a grouping of sofas and armchairs, between which were placed small side-tables on pedestals.

'Turn around just about here,' she said, standing in the centre of a garland of roses on the fine Aubusson carpet. 'Then walk back out of the smaller side door over there.'

The girls gave a practice walk before returning to the dressing room which was filled with racks of clothes, each of which had the model's name on it. A young woman called Clarisse was assigned to do Nathalie's make-up and hair. She sat her in front of a large mirror and sorted through her large box of cosmetics for the right shade. Nathalie was beginning to enjoy this pampering. It was a far cry from her life with the Reynauds and the Résistance.

Clarisse was a friendly, talkative girl, and seeing that the other two models were occupied in conversation, Nathalie thought it was a good chance to do a little prying.

'Have you been working for the Monsieur long?' she asked.

'Since the war. It was Mme Lefort who found me. I was working for Mademoiselle Chanel until then.'

'Is it true what they say about her? Does she really have a German lover?'

Clarisse smiled. 'It's common knowledge. She divides her time between rue Cambon and the Ritz.'

'Most of the couturiers shut up shop when the Germans arrived, I believe.' You were lucky to find this job – as was I?'

Clarisse asked Nathalie to close her eyes whilst she applied a shade of silvery-brown eye shadow with a brush. 'I can tell by your accent you're not from Paris. Where are you from?'

'A small village near the Pyrénées. Not far from...'

'What brought you here?'

'I came to stay with my uncle and look for work.'

'Did you find anything – before this job I mean?'

I worked in their flower shop for a while, but they were struggling to pay me. That's when I found this work.'

Clarisse stood back to check Nathalie's eyes. When she was

satisfied, she started on her eyebrows, brushing them into a fine curve with a dark brown crayon.

There was so much Nathalie wanted to ask, but she knew she had to tread carefully. *It's now or never,* she said to herself.

'Do you know Lucien Chambrun?' she asked. 'It was he who got me the job.'

Clarisse finished the eyebrows and then started on her hair. For a minute, Nathalie thought she wasn't going to answer.

'Lucien Chambrun! No I don't know anyone called Chambrun. What does he look like?'

Nathalie tried to describe him, but Clarisse still had no idea who she meant. Pierre had been so sure Chambrun was François Corneille. If so, why had he lied to her?

The door opened and Mme Lefort entered. The soft sounds of a pianist playing a Beethoven Sonata in the salon drifted into the room.

'You have ten minutes, girls,' said the vendeuse. She turned to Clarisse and told her to help Nathalie dress.

'Do you happen to know the people we will be modelling for?' Nathalie asked, as she held up her arms for Clarisse to slip a silk dress over her head. 'It's just that as it's my first time, I am rather nervous.'

Clarisse checked to see that the other two girls were out of earshot. 'We are told not to discuss the clients,' she whispered, 'but if it will put you at ease, then I'll tell you.'

She reeled off a list of names. Baron Gunter von Schwartzburg, from the German High Command in Paris; Heinrich Wertheimer, who was here from Warsaw; Dieter Fischer, a friend of SS General Walther Schellenberg, Count Antonio Albani, from the Italian Foreign Office, and Ambrus Gabor, an Austro-Hungarian official from Vienna.

'The Countess Irené is also here,' she added. 'She's one of the Monsieur's favourites and usually comes with her young lover, Daniel. The midnight blue dress is for her. But don't worry, they will barely notice you. They are here for the dresses.'

Nathalie tried hard to memorise all the names.

When the time came for the showing, Mme Lefort stood by the door as the girls paraded into the salon, one at a time. Nathalie was the last. She would have to do this four more times with another four changes of clothes. After the second time, she felt confident enough to steal a quick glance at some of the clients. She had no idea who was who, but was able to make a mental note of their looks. Among them was the same woman she had seen the day she came for her interview. She had brought the Pekinese dog with her again.

Afterwards, each girl was given a list of the dresses selected for them to model again. This time they were to stay in the salon for each client to take a closer look. Nathalie was told she only had one to model – the midnight blue, silk dress. Clarisse helped her slip into it, tidied up her hair, and checked her make-up.

Nathalie returned to the salon and was relieved to find the atmosphere less formal. Several guests were helping themselves to food, and the piano music had been replaced with more upbeat, big band gramophone records. She was directed to the woman with the Pekinese, who passed the dog on to a man whilst she looked at the dress.

'It's magnificent, Jacques,' she said, in a soft dulcet voice. 'Absolutely exquisite.' She felt the fabric whilst De Rossier pointed out particular elements of the cutting technique that enhanced the fabric and line.

'What do you think, Daniel?' she asked, 'Don't you agree that it will go so well with my sapphires, or the pearls.'

By now, Nathalie realised the woman was none other than the Countess Irené. Daniel told her what she wanted to hear; that the dress was made for her and she must buy it. De Rossier was beside himself with delight.

Nathalie was about to leave the salon when something unexpected happened.

'Daniel,' the Countess said. 'This young lady looks exactly like the woman in the portrait, the one that you gave me a few weeks ago.' She drew an imaginary line around Nathalie's neck. 'Just imagine that this lady is wearing a string of pearls and is wearing her hair down. She even has the same eyes.' The man didn't answer. Much to Nathalie's embarrassment, the Countess continued. 'My dear, have you ever had your portrait painted?'

Nathalie was so worked up, she lost her voice. The Countess apologised for embarrassing her and turned back to the man. 'The woman in the portrait is wearing a simple dress though – almost dowdy. Such a coincidence, don't you think?'

Nathalie was told she could leave, but before doing so, stole a quick glance towards the man called Daniel. Tall, tanned, and impeccably dressed, he was simply, one of the most handsome men she'd ever laid eyes on. To add to his startling looks, he stood in such a way, that the filtered light streaming through the window made him look as though he'd stepped out of a Renaissance masterpiece. Nathalie's eyes fell on his shoes – elegant nut-brown leather with black edging at the seams; bespoke shoes of distinction that could only have been made for someone with money and good taste. It was easy to see how the Countess had fallen for such a man.

Clarisse had left when Nathalie returned to the dressing room and it was far too risky to ask the other girls any questions about the Countess. Overcome by a wave of nausea, she sat in front of the mirror fighting back the tears whilst she cleaned off her makeup. This could only mean one thing – if it was her portrait they were talking about, then Pierre must have sold the painting to him. Her mind was a whirlpool of confusion. Pierre knew who Chambrun was, *and* he painted a portrait that sounded exactly like the one the Countess was referring to. It was too much of a coincidence.

Mme Lefort came into the dressing room to congratulate her. 'Well done, Nathalie. Monsieur is most pleased with you.' She handed her another pay packet. This time it was even more than the last one – several hundred francs.

'When would you like to see me again?' Nathalie asked.

'In a week's time; if we need you before then, we have your telephone number.'

A crushing anxiety now enveloped her. What should have been a good day was now marred with the sickening thought that Pierre had sold her portrait to the Countess's lover. She stopped at a bar on the way home and ordered a cognac, whilst mulling over what to do next. Her instinct was to confront Pierre. He said the man had paid a substantial amount of money. Daniel certainly could have afforded it. How was he to know it would end up being a gift for the Countess? *Pure coincidence*, she said to herself.

Deep down, Nathalie knew the right thing to do was to tell Paul. After all, he was in charge of the network and he specifically said he wanted to know who De Rossier's guests were. But would he laugh at her when she told him about the painting? He might even be angry with her for spending so much time with another member of the network. She remembered that Pierre had also asked her to tell him who would be there. Maybe that would give her an excuse to see his reaction. In the end, the decision was made for her.

CHAPTER THIRTEEN

Paul was waiting for Nathalie at *La Vie en Fleurs*.

'Let's go for a drink,' he said. 'You can tell me all about your day.'

He took her to a small bar in rue Frédéric Chopin with a clear view of Café Voltaire. Unlike the fashionable café, which was filled with customers, this bar was empty.

'I can tell by the look on your face, today didn't go too well. Did you slip in those fancy shoes,' he asked, with a smile.

At first, Nathalie felt too overwhelmed to speak, but after the cognac, she could no longer hide her feelings.

'I slipped,' she replied. 'But not in that way.'

'Do you want to talk about it?'

Her eyes glistened with tears as she told him what took place, starting with the names of those who attended, and the incident with the painting. The look on his face gave nothing away.

'The Countess is quite famous in Parisian high society,' Paul replied, lighting up a Gitane. 'More for her pro-German feelings than anything else, so it's hardly a surprise that she should be there. This new lover of hers is Daniel Corneille. He works for the B.M.A.'

Nathalie face paled. 'He wouldn't happen to be the son of François Corneille, would he?'

Paul looked hard in to her eyes. 'Was he there also?'

She let out a deep sigh and rubbed her temples.

'I have a feeling it was François Corneille that I met over there,' she inclined her head towards Café Voltaire. 'I was at *Le Lapin Agile* with Pierre one evening, and he happened to be there with a young woman. Pierre told me his real name. I wasn't sure whether or not to believe him. Now I'm beginning to think Lucien Chambrun never existed.'

Paul surprised her by saying that he'd already guessed it was him at the café. He called the bar owner over.

'Marcel, can you tell us who you saw Nathalie with, a few weeks ago?'

Marcel swung his red and white check tea towel over his shoulder and poured them another drink on the house. 'François Corneille,' he replied, matter-of-factly. 'I'd know that *mouchard* anywhere.'

Nathalie was too ashamed to look Paul in the face. She had committed the gravest sin any Résistance member could do. She'd probably compromised the network by taking the new job.

'I should leave immediately,' she said. 'Go back to the Pyrénées.'

'You weren't to know,' Paul replied. 'Marcel works for us. It was he who told us Corneille had been seen in the area and we guessed he was on the lookout for people he could recruit as a collaborator. No doubt he intended to make sure you became accustomed to the finer things in life before he swooped and tried to compromise you – an eagle with its prey.'

Nathalie thought of René. 'I could have jeopardized the assignment.'

'You didn't. That's all that mattered.'

'Do you think they've been following me?'

'We have to consider it's a possibility, although up to now you have shown yourself to be the model citizen. They have nothing on you.' His face grew anxious. 'No my dear, it's not you I'm worried about. It's Pierre.'

Nathalie's eyes widened. 'What are you trying to say?'

'We don't know for sure that the portrait Daniel gave to the Countess *is* the same one Pierre painted of you, but we can find out.'

'And if it is?'

'We will cross that bridge when we come to it. Leave it with me.' He leaned across the table and patted her hand like a child. 'For the moment, carry on as normal and promise me one thing – that you won't contact Pierre.'

'I give you my word.'

'Good girl. Now,' he said, getting up to leave, 'we'd better be getting back to the Reynauds. They will have dinner prepared.'

A few days later, Nathalie received a call to meet Paul at a bistro near the Pont de l'Alma.

'The news is not good,' he declared despondently. 'The portrait is definitely of you.'

Nathalie felt a feeling of nausea in the pit of her stomach.

'How did you find out?' she asked, miserably.

'It's common knowledge that the Countess lives in a fashionable apartment near the Élysée Palace. We managed to get two of our men inside the apartment disguised as plumbers. They turned off the water mains to the building, and then asked to inspect the pipes. Your painting is hanging in her hallway. I gave them one of your photographs, so there was no mistake. Pierre's signature is also on it. You know what this means, don't you?'

'That you think Pierre is somehow involved.'

'For a while now, I've suspected there could be a traitor in our midst. After the first raid, when Anna was killed, I suspected everyone – even the Reynauds. Only Gilbert escaped that raid and I was sure it wasn't him.'

'How did you come to that conclusion?' Nathalie asked.

'Gilbert is a rough character but he would never betray his friends. He's been with us from the start and has always shown great loyalty. Besides, he was also in love with Anna. The idea that he would put her in danger doesn't make sense.'

Gilbert in love with Anna! Nathalie couldn't believe what she was hearing.

'I never knew that,' she said. 'Pierre didn't mention it.'

'He wouldn't. They were rivals for her love. In the end, Pierre won.'

'What about the other raid? When Sylvie was caught and tortured. Do you have any idea what went wrong there.'

Paul shook his head. 'Somehow, the Germans got wind of the operation. Thank God, they didn't find us at the Pont de l'Alma.'

'How does Pierre fit into all this?' Nathalie asked. 'Are you saying he's a traitor just because he sold a painting to someone from the Bureau of Anti-National activities?'

Paul shrugged his shoulder. 'I'm not sure how he came to be mixed up with them, but it can't be ignored.'

Nathalie didn't need to ask what would happen if they found out he'd betrayed them. The consequences didn't bear thinking about. Again, Paul warned her to stay away from him.

Towards the end of the week, she met Paul at the deserted warehouse for more target practice. Nathalie was shocked at his appearance. He appeared to have aged ten years and was a shadow of his former self. She was in no doubt that it was the worry about a traitor that had caused this. He told her that the Allies were intending to make a landing sometime within the next year. Because of this, there had been more parachute drops of weapons and ammunition for the Maquis and the Résistance. All this meant their activities had to be stepped up.

'In a few weeks, there'll be another important mission,' he

said. 'I can't say any more at this point. I'm sure you understand why.'

'And Pierre?' she asked. 'Will he be involved?'

At the mention of his name, Paul became agitated and changed the conversation back to her shooting practice. 'Now try this one,' he said, and handed her a machine gun.

CHAPTER FOURTEEN

Nathalie was helping Mme Reynaud arrange flowers outside *La Vie en Fleurs* when a call came through from Paul. It was Antoine who took the coded message. He put the phone down and hurried outside. The two women could see by the look on his face it was important.

'What is it?' asked Mme Reynaud, anxiously.

'Things are on the move. Paul wants Nathalie to meet him at Marcel's bar in ten minutes.'

Three weeks had passed since Nathalie last saw him. Since then she had not been given any assignments in case she was being followed. Thankfully, boredom was relieved with her work at the atelier. Altogether, there had been four more private showings. All had gone well and much to her relief, neither the Countess, nor Daniel, had attended. Neither had she seen the elusive "Chambrun".

She hurried to the bar. Paul was waiting for her. Nathalie asked if anyone else would be joining them.

'Only one more.' He looked at the large clock on the wall. 'Let's hope he arrives soon.'

Nathalie prayed that person would be Pierre and she felt a

huge disappointment when she saw Gilbert cross the road. She could not bear to look at him.

Marcel brought over a platter of toast, hard cheese, coffee and cognac, and Paul started to outline their mission.

'In two hours, we will be moving another "package" –three agents sent by the Free French. They are to be transported by car to a place on the outskirts of Paris where they will be met by another group and taken to a destination in the countryside.

'Where is this place?' Gilbert asked.

'It's a church – Saint-Michel – situated at the end of the tree lined Place Alboni. Catch the Metro to Passy and it will be on your right as you exit. At exactly 12:30 p.m. two men wearing Milice uniforms will arrive and park outside the church door. They will be in a black Citroen.' He turned to Gilbert. 'There's a safe house near the church – number 74. Make your way there. Someone will let you in. Your job is to keep watch. The car will only stop for a few minutes; long enough to collect the men inside the church. If there is a problem, you must make sure the curtains are closed, in which case the car will not stop.'

Paul turned his attention to Nathalie. 'Your job is to pick up important documents from them before they leave. Any questions?'

The mission seemed simple enough. It was not the first time the group had used a car and men dressed in *Milice* uniform. They had done this many times before and each time was successful.

'I don't want you going together,' Paul continued. 'Make your own way there. Gilbert, you will go first.'

'Fine,' Gilbert replied, 'in which case I'd better get a move on.'

He got up and shook Paul's hand.

'Good luck, my friend,' Paul said.

Gilbert turned to Nathalie. 'I will see you there.'

Every operation was dangerous, no matter how small, yet he didn't betray any emotion. His eyes were stone cold.

Nathalie felt a mild irritation towards Paul at being asked to do an operation with a man she detested, but she refrained from speaking out. Paul watched Gilbert walk down the street. As soon as he was out of sight, he motioned to Marcel to make a telephone call. The telephone was in an alcove behind the bar making it impossible to hear the conversation. Seconds later, he returned giving Paul a nod. This obvious sign language between the two of them alarmed Nathalie whose nerves were already on edge at having to take part in an operation with Gilbert.

'I'd better be going also,' she said, making a move to leave.

Paul reached out and grabbed her hand.

'Sit down. There's been a change of plan.'

Nathalie stared at him in disbelief, wondering if this wasn't as a result of the mysterious phone call.

'I don't understand,' she said, knitting her brows together. 'Is something wrong?'

Sometime around midday, Nathalie walked into a second-hand bookstore on the Avenue de New York. This broad street, with its sweeping view of the Seine, was a place she had come to know well over the past year. The bookshop was not far from the Pont de l'Alma. After perusing the narrow aisles, she eventually picked up a book of short stories by Guy de Maupassant. When she presented it to the man at the cashier's desk, he glanced around the shop and told her to follow him. At the back of the shop amidst shelves of old magazines, was a door that opened into a hallway with a dark, narrow staircase leading down to the cellar.

The man switched on his flashlight. 'Down there,' he said. 'Mind the steps.'

When she entered the cellar, Nathalie was more than relieved to see half a dozen other members of the network already there, including Mme Reynaud. They were busily emptying crates of ammunition and weapons.

'Where's Antoine?' Nathalie asked Mme Reynaud.

'Paul sent him elsewhere. That's all I know. There's a lot happening and he's keeping things close to his chest. Paul won't be coming tonight either.'

Before she could ask any more, one of the men put her to work, unloading the crates. 'Make a note of the contents,' he said, handing her a pad and pen. 'And be careful: we don't want to get blown up.

During the next few hours, the contents of the crates had all been accounted for. It was the biggest concealment of arms and ammunition she'd ever seen. All of it had come from the Special Operations Executive in London, and was intended for distribution to the various Résistance networks.

By nine o'clock the sun started to set, sending narrow shafts of golden light between the iron bars of the small window that looked out at eye level onto the avenue. The basement became darker and in no time they could barely see each other. Now they had to sit and wait. The continuous wail of sirens penetrated the room. Several convoys of armoured vehicles rumbled along the avenue followed closely by lines of motorcycles. The Germans were out in force, and it didn't bode well for their operation. Just before curfew, the sound of footsteps running along the pavement made them reach for their guns. The footsteps came to a halt outside the bookshop, which had long closed its doors. Nathalie had her small Polish pistol tucked away in the back of her trousers. She pulled it out, praying she wouldn't need to use it. One of the men cocked his pistol and stood on a crate to see who it was. He heard the bookstore door open and the men disappeared inside. Everyone was on tenterhooks.

A few minutes later, the footsteps reached the basement. Nathalie could hear the deafening sound of her heart beating wildly in her chest. The door opened and a man shone a flashlight at them.

She let out a shocked gasp. It was Pierre. With him were six men, who by the look on their faces were as relieved as they were to be amongst friends. Pierre introduced them as representatives of General De Gaulle's Free French and they were about to make the same journey out of Paris that others had made – by coal barge; the same barge that had brought the cache of arms the night before.

Pierre settled himself down next to Nathalie. '*Bon soir,* my friend,' he said.

Even in the darkness of the cellar, she could make out a tentative smile. There was so much she wanted to ask him, but now was not the right time.

At the stroke of midnight, the men prepared to make their way to the waiting barge. Nathalie left the cellar with everyone else to keep a lookout. It was much easier to move seasoned men in the field than it was ordinary civilians, and it wasn't long before the men were well hidden in the barge. In the absence of Paul, the man in charge was the same one who had told Nathalie to make a list of the contents of the cache. He counted out a wad of money for the captain and they shook hands. There was a collective sigh of relief as they watched the barge quietly slip out of the shadows under the Pont de l'Alma and travel up the Seine. All had gone well. The "package" was on its way and the group congratulated each other. They returned to the safety of the cellar where they had been told to wait for further instructions.

The ebullient mood did not last. In the morning, Paul arrived. Except for those who were to stay behind and attend to the removal of the guns and ammunition, everyone else was told to make their way to the warehouse used for target practice. Nathalie left with him. Throughout the one-hour journey, he did not utter a single word and appeared to be in a world of his own, which alarmed her.

At the warehouse, Nathalie got the shock of her life. Inside were at least thirty armed résistants. The fact that they were dangerously gathered together in one spot spoke volumes. Something serious had taken place.

The résistants moved aside and Paul made his way towards a table in the centre of the group. He took a seat alongside two other men. A hush descended over the crowd and Paul began to speak.

'I've brought you all here to pass judgement on the man who almost brought us undone,' he said, and waved his hand towards the back of the warehouse.

A scuffle broke out and two men dragged a man forward through the crowd. They sat him on a chair some metres away from the table, and tied him securely with rope. The man's head was bloodied and beaten and flopped down over his chest. One of the men grabbed him by the hair and held his head back for everyone to see.

Nathalie bit her lip to stop herself crying out. It was Gilbert.

'This man,' Paul continued, with a sweeping arm gesture, 'is someone I have known since before the Germans arrived. It shames me to say that he is a *mouchard* of the worst kind. It was he who informed the Gestapo of the escape which saw some of our members and escapees killed, including Anna Benesh.'

Nathalie glanced towards Pierre who stood staring at the ground.

'Having sold his soul to the devil, he betrayed us again. The next time Sylvie was taken and executed.' Paul paused for a moment in order for everyone to digest the enormity of his speech. 'At this point you might wonder why we were not all raided and hauled to Avenue Foch. But the Gestapo are clever. They wanted us to sweat. Next, this wretched man was asked to betray someone else close to us all. That man was Pierre. Why, I hear you ask? Because he held a grudge against him for falling in love with a woman he himself was in love with, scorned love that could have brought us all down. At first, Pierre's parents were harassed by the Gestapo in their village, and when they refused to give their son away, even under torture, he was visited at his apartment in Montmartre by a member of the Bureau of Anti-National Activities. Pierre refused to give anyone away. Unfortunately, that man bought a painting for his mistress. Before he could give it to her, his father saw it and went in search of the woman. In all likelihood, it was to recruit her too. We shall never know.'

By this time, Nathalie thought her legs would give way. Mme Reynaud came closer to her and looped her arm through hers, giving her an assuring squeeze.

Paul continued. 'We followed these men for several weeks. Now I can assure you all that as from last night, this threat was eliminated. In the early hours of the morning, two of our men entered the apartment of the Countess Irené Moreau-Kaminski. She was eliminated in her bed, along with her lover, Daniel Corneille. Some hours prior to this, Corneille's father, one of the most senior men in the Bureau of Anti-National Activities, was also eliminated by a lone gunman, as he left the offices to go home. The only one who remains is this man. Yesterday, there was to be an assignment at the Place Alboni. Only myself and two others knew about this. One of them was later given another assignment. The other – this man who sits before you – notified the Gestapo as soon as he left the meeting. Knowing full well the crime he had committed, he entered his assigned destination, but we were waiting for him. We brought him here only minutes before the area was surrounded.'

Paul stopped for a moment to gauge the looks on everyone's faces. Their eyes shone with hatred.

'It is you who will pass judgement on this man today. Think carefully about what he has done.'

After a few minutes of silence, Paul asked the men to vote on Gilbert's guilt.

'All those who believe this man is not guilty, raise your hand.'

Not a single hand was raised.

'All those who believe this man guilty, raise your hand.'

This time everyone raised their hand including Nathalie.

Paul asked Gilbert if he had anything to say. He refused to answer.

Nathalie held her breath. Everyone in the room knew what would happen next. Paul picked up his pistol which had been lying on the table, and cocked it. He walked over to Gilbert, pressed it to his temple, and fired. A gush of red spurted from his head and he slumped forward. Nathalie realised she had been gripping Mme Reynaud's arm so tightly, her arm had become numb. In that moment, she felt a surge of nausea and vomited.

ugust 1944

A Nathalie opened the shutters and looked at the majestic peaks of Pyrénées in the distance, a landscape of towering summits, plateaus, valleys and meadows. It wasn't until she returned home that she realized how much she'd missed them. For four years, the hiking trails had seen some of the most arduous escapes in the war. Hundreds had passed along them in search of freedom, braving the harshest of winters with below zero temperatures and howling gales. Now the tracks had fallen silent.

It was almost a year since she returned back to her village and she remembered it as if it was yesterday. After all, coming back was not what she'd anticipated. She'd always expected to be in Paris when the Allies landed. The decision for her to return was not hers to make. It was Paul's. Her new assignment was to take charge of "packages" escaping into Spain.

After the events leading up to Gilbert's execution, it was no longer safe to be in Paris. The Gestapo would leave no stone unturned until everyone in the network was caught. Whilst Gilbert's body was unceremoniously being dumped in the Seine, Nathalie was given travel documents under a false name, and told to leave Paris immediately. The Reynauds were also advised to leave to an unknown destination in the country. *La Vie en Fleurs* was boarded up and they left straight away.

There was one thing Nathalie needed to do before she departed. Unbeknown to Paul, she returned the fine clothes to the rue du Faubourg Saint-Honoré saying she had decided to leave Paris and that she appreciated the kindness of the Monsieur to give her work in times of hardship. She was told that both De Rossier and Mme Lefort were attending the funerals of close friends. Nathalie was in no doubt as to whose they were. She left the premises with mixed feelings. On the one hand, meeting Corneille had flushed out the traitor in their midst; on the other, she had worked with collaborators. And then there was Pierre. He could not let go of Anna's memory and he left Paris. She never saw him again.

Nathalie heard her mother call. 'Get a move on or you'll miss the train.'

She pulled out her battered brown suitcase from the closet and started to pack. Her pistol was still inside it. She took it out and looked at it. In all that time, she had never needed to use it. Paul had told her that once she killed someone, it would never leave her. Thankfully, she would never know. She placed it in the drawer, finished packing, and went downstairs for a bite to eat before leaving.

Her father was sitting at the kitchen table reading the newspaper.

'There were times when I never thought France would be liberated,' he said, his voice quivering with emotion.

'I know, Papa,' Nathalie replied. 'I felt the same.'

'How long will you be gone this time?' her mother asked.

'Maybe a week: two at the most.'

The scene at the train station was a far cry from the one she'd experienced the last time she left. A band was playing the Marseillaise and throngs of happy families were being united with their loved ones. She bought a copy of *Paris Match* and boarded the train back to Paris. This time her trip was for a different reason. Paul had asked her to be with him when they welcomed Général de Gaulle back to Paris. She could not have been happier.

In Paris, the jubilant crowds in the streets took her breath away. The hated Nazi swastika had been replaced with thousands of French flags. Bands were playing, people were dancing, and strangers were hugging and kissing each other. Paul emerged through the crowd to meet her.

'Welcome back to Paris,' he said, handing her a bouquet of roses. 'A welcome-back gift from us all, courtesy of *La Vie en Fleurs.*'

'How are the Reynauds?' Nathalie asked.

'Much better now that they are back in the shop again. They're looking forward to seeing you.'

Nathalie and Paul arrived at the War Ministry just in time to hear Général de Gaulle's rousing speech. It was the moment the whole of France had waited for.

'*Vive La France!*' he shouted at the end. The crowd went wild.

Vive la France! France is free again.

The crowds began to move aside as a procession of armoured vehicles passed by. Nathalie froze when she recognized one of the occupants' faces.

'*Mon Dieu!*' she cried, grabbing Paul's arm. 'Look who it is.'

For a brief moment she stood, remembering the man who had walked out of her life in Tours, leaving her with a warm glow. Now here he was again. She threw up her hands and waved at him.

'René!' she called out. 'René!'

René had also seen her and he told the driver to stop the vehicle.

'Camille,' he shouted out, reaching his arm out towards her. In one swift movement, he pulled her on to the vehicle beside him.

'René,' she laughed, her eyes filled with tears.

He kissed her full on the lips. 'In my darkest days, I never thought I'd see you again.'

'Nor I you,' she said, tears streaming down her cheeks.

'A new era has begun,' he said, pressing her close to him. 'And this time I'm not going to let you get away.'

The End

If you've enjoyed Camille and would like more espionage adventures, please have a look at 'Conspiracy of Lies' Here.

If you would be so kind as to leave an honest review on Amazon, please do so Here. It can make such a difference and would be greatly appriciated

ABOUT THE AUTHOR

Kathryn Gauci was born in Leicestershire, England, and studied textile design at Loughborough College of Art and later at Kidderminster College of Art and Design where she specialised in carpet design and technology. After graduating, Kathryn spent a year in Vienna, Austria before moving to Greece. She worked as a carpet designer in Athens for six years before eventually settling in Melbourne, Australia, where she ran her own textile design studio in Melbourne for over fifteen years. *The Embroiderer* is her first novel; a culmination of those wonderful years of design and travel, and especially of those glorious years in her youth living and working in Greece.

Her second novel, *Conspiracy of Lies*, set in France during WWII is based on the stories of real life agents in the service of the Special Operations Executive and the Resistance under Nazi occupied Europe. To put one's life on the line for your country in the pursuit of freedom took immense courage and many never survived. Kathryn's interest in WWII started when she lived in Vienna and has continued ever since. She is a regular visitor to France and has spent time in several of the areas in which this novel is set. *Conspiracy of Lies* is the recipient of several literary awards including 'chillwithabook' Book of the Year 2017

ALSO BY KATHRYN GAUCI

WWII

Conspiracy of Lies

Code Name Camille

The Asia Minor Trilogy

The Embroiderer

Seraphina's Song

The Carpet Weaver of Usak

See below for Book Descriptions

Conspiracy of Lies:

A powerful account of one woman's struggle to balance her duty to her country and a love she knows will ultimately end in tragedy. *Which would you choose?*

1940. The Germans are about to enter Paris, Claire Bouchard flees for England. Two years later she is sent back to work alongside the Resistance.

Working undercover as a teacher in Brittany, Claire accidentally befriends the wife of the German Commandant of Rennes and the blossoming friendship is about to become a dangerous mission.

Knowing thousands of lives depend on her actions, Claire begins a double life as a Gestapo Commandant's mistress in order to retrieve vital information for the Allies, but ghosts from her past make the deception more painful than she could have imagined.

A time of horror, yet amongst so much strength and love Conspiracy of Lies takes us on a journey through occupied France, from the picturesque villages of rural Brittany to the glittering dinner parties of the Nazi elite.

Take a trip back to a time of overwhelming strength and courage.

The Embroiderer:

A richly woven saga set against the mosques and minarets of Asia Minor and the ruins of ancient Athens.

1822: As The Greek War of Independence rages, a child is born to a woman of legendary beauty on the Greek island of Chios. The subsequent decades of bitter struggle between Greeks and Turks simmer to a head when the Greek army invades Turkey in 1919. During this time, Dimitra Lamartine arrives in Smyrna and gains fame and fortune as an embroiderer to the elite of Ottoman society. However, it is her granddaughter, Sophia, who takes the business to great heights as a couturier in Constantinople only to see their world come crashing down with the outbreak of war.

1922: Sophia begins a new life in Athens, but the memory of a dire prophecy once told to her grandmother about a girl with flaming red hair begins to haunt her with devastating consequences with the occupation of Greece by the Axis Powers in 1941

1972: Eleni Stephenson is called to the bedside of her dying aunt in Athens. In a story that rips her world apart, Eleni discovers the chilling truth behind her family's dark past plunging her into the shadowy world of political intrigue, secret societies and espionage where families and friends are torn apart and where a belief in superstition simmers just below the surface.

Extravagant, inventive, emotionally sweeping, The Embroiderer is a tale that travellers and those who seek culture and oriental history will love.

The Carpet Weaver of Usak:

"Springtime and early summer are always beautiful in Anatolia. Hardy winter crocuses, blooming in their thousands, are followed by blue muscari which adorn the meadows like glorious sapphires on a silk carpet."

A haunting story of a deep friendship between two women, one Greek, one Turk. A friendship that transcends an era of mistrust, and fear, long after the wars have ended.

Aspasia and Saniye are friends from childhood. They share their secrets and joy, helping each other in times of trouble.

When WWII breaks, the news travels to the village, but the locals have no idea how it will affect their lives.

When the war ends the Greeks come to the village, causing havoc, burning houses and shooting Turks. The residents regard each other with suspicion. Their world has turned upside down, but some of the old friendships survive, despite the odds.

But the Greeks are finally defeated, and the situation changes once more, forcing the Greeks to leave the country. Yet, the friendship between the villagers still continues.

Many years later, in Athens, Christophorus tells his grandson, and his daughter, Elpida, the missing parts of the story, and what he had to leave behind in Asia Minor.

A story of love, friendship, and loss; a tragedy that affects the lives of many on both sides of the Aegean, and their struggle to survive under new circumstances, as casualties of a war beyond their control.

Seraphina's Song:

Dionysos is a man without a future, a man who embraces destiny and risks everything for love.

"If I knew then, dear reader, what I know now, I should have turned on my heels and left. But I stood transfixed on the beautiful image of Seraphina. In that moment my fate was sealed."

A refugee who escapes Smyrna in 1922 disguised as an old woman. Alienated and plagued by remorse, he spirals into poverty and seeks solace in the hashish dens of Piraeus.

When he can go no lower, opportunity knocks, and Dionysos' meets Aleko, an expert bouzouki player, recognising a rare musical talent, Aleko offers to teach him to play.

But Dionysos' hope for a better life unravels when he meets Seraphina — the singer with the voice of a nightingale. From that moment his life is in danger and there is no going back.

"Cine noir meets Greek tragedy, played out with a depression era realism." Discovering Diamonds

A haunting and compelling story of hope and despair, and of a love stronger than death.

For more information and updates, please subscribe to my newsletter through my author website here.

Printed by Amazon Italia Logistica S.r.l.
Torrazza Piemonte (TO), Italy

12673828R00066